Carrie

Brooker Baptist Church
839-4953

Distributed By
CHOICE BOOKS
50 KENT AVE.
KITCHENER, ONT.
N2G 3R1
We Welcome Your Response

HEARTSONG BOOKS

Carrie

Carole Gift Page

BETHANY HOUSE PUBLISHERS
MINNEAPOLIS, MINNESOTA 55438
A Division of Bethany Fellowship, Inc.

CAROLE GIFT PAGE is a free-lance writer, part-time writing instructor and conference speaker living in Garden Grove, California. She was born in Michigan, married in 1966, and is the mother of three children. Mrs. Page attended Jackson Junior College and graduated from Bob Jones University with a B.S. degree in art education. She is a longtime member of First Baptist Church of Lakewood in Long Beach, California. She has also written *Kara* for the Heartsong Books series.

Library of Congress Catalog Card Number 84–71699

ISBN 0–87123–441–6

Copyright © 1984
Carole Gift Page
All Rights Reserved

Published by Bethany House Publishers
A Division of Bethany Fellowship, Inc.
6820 Auto Club Road, Minneapolis, Minnesota 55438

Printed in the United States of America

DEDICATION

Devotedly, to my Grandmother Gift who made more things
possible for me than she will ever know.

Other books you will want to read:

SPRINGFLOWER BOOKS (13–15):
Lisa
Melissa
Michelle
Sara

HEARTSONG BOOKS (for young adults):
Andrea
Jenny
Kara
Karen
Anne

Chapter One

Today is the wedding.

That was Carrie Seyers' first thought on that bright, lilac-scented June morning. That afternoon Kara Strickland and Greg Arlen would become husband and wife. For Carrie, it meant that her half sister would be marrying the only man Carrie had ever loved.

For over two years Carrie had tried to convince herself that losing Greg didn't matter. He had never really been hers anyway, never even suspected the depth of her feelings for him. They had been nothing more than childhood friends. So why did she feel so devastated now?

After several reluctant moments, Carrie forced herself out of bed, splashed water on her face, and brushed her teeth. In the early morning light, her round, rosy face seemed sallow and her blue-gray eyes shadowed.

I look awful, she thought dismally. Even her thick chestnut-brown hair that always framed her face attractively appeared limp and lifeless today. *It's all in your head,* she chided herself. It was true. Her spirits were dragging on the floor. She felt sluggish, as if she were moving in slow motion. She was out of sync with the day, with herself, with the entire world.

She had secretly hoped to awaken this morning and find herself ill—a high fever, perhaps, or a contagious bout of flu. Anything for an excuse to miss the wedding, to avoid standing beside Kara as her maid of honor or watching while her father, Wilson Seyers, gave Kara to Greg with his blessings. But here she was, disgustingly healthy—except for that deep, persistent pain of yearning for Greg. There was no cure for that.

The hardest task today would be facing people. Some knew of her feelings for Greg; others didn't. But *she* knew. She dreaded even going to the breakfast table this morning and facing her parents and brother. *They* knew. They never said anything directly, but she had seen the covert glances and recognized the veiled concern in their voices when they talked of the marriage.

Summoning courage she wasn't sure she had, Carrie put on her robe and slippers and padded to the kitchen. Her mother was at the stove frying bacon. The rich aromas of bacon, coffee, and hot cinnamon rolls should have been tempting.

"Good morning, dear," said her mother, looking up and smiling. Lynn Seyers' warm green eyes held a question: *How are you, and how will you handle today?*

Carrie looked away, ignoring the unspoken inquiry. She picked up the rolls and butter and carried them to the table, joining her father and brother.

"Great! Here comes the chow. It's about time, woman!" said red-headed, freckle-faced Danny. Sometimes he behaved like fifteen instead of eighteen.

Any other time Carrie would have shot back a flippant remark, but today she dismissed Danny's teasing with a withering glance, then sat down.

"Hello, sweetheart," greeted her father, looking up from his paper. Wilson Seyers, an attractive man with auburn-blond hair and an easy smile, was editor of the *Claremont News,* yet he read each edition religiously, as if every word were new.

"Hi, Dad," said Carrie, forcing a smile.

Her mother placed a platter of bacon and scrambled eggs on the table and sat down across from Carrie. Lynn wore a crisp bone-white pantsuit and her shining brown hair was immaculate. "Would you ask the blessing, dear?" she asked.

Carrie bowed her head and offered a hurried thank-you for the food. Guiltily she realized she should have asked God's blessing on Kara and Greg's marriage, but she simply couldn't bring herself to say the words.

As Danny helped himself to the scrambled eggs, he said brightly, "Well, today's the big day. Our dear half sister finally gets her man."

"Danny, you're so crude," snapped Carrie.

"Well, sourpuss, I haven't noticed you exactly dancing a jig around here lately. I thought weddings were such a big deal for girls."

"Danny, you're impossible!"

"Hey, hey, you two," interrupted Wilson. "This is a big day. Let's not spoil it by bickering."

"You bet it's a big day," returned Danny. "I gotta wear one of those ridiculous monkey suits in this heat—and it's not even my own wedding!"

Lynn smiled at Danny. "When all the girls see you in your tuxedo, they'll be lining up for blocks."

"Yeah, sure. They'll be lining up for a good laugh," he snickered.

Wilson gave his daughter a searching look. "How are you today, Carrie?"

"Fine," she replied, too quickly.

"You're sure?"

"Yes. Why wouldn't I be?"

"I mean, now that Kara's wedding day is actually here . . ."

"I'm happy for Greg and her, Daddy."

"It's about time those two tied the knot," interjected Danny. "They've been engaged for over two years."

"They were wise to wait," replied Wilson. "Kara was able to complete her education and care for her mother until she recovered from that terrible fire. I think both Kara and Greg have shown an impressive sense of maturity and responsibility."

Carrie pushed back her chair and stood up. "Excuse me. I have lots to do."

"You didn't eat anything," observed her mother with concern.

"I'm not hungry," replied Carrie. "Besides, I've got to make sure the hem of my dress is even, and I promised Kara I'd wrap her gifts for the bridesmaids. You know we've got to be at the church in just a couple of hours."

"Don't sweat it," scoffed Danny. "Everybody always gets frantic before a wedding, but the ceremony always comes off without a hitch."

Carrie turned abruptly and hurried to her room before anyone could see her tears and realize this was one wedding she didn't want to see happen at all.

Chapter Two

That night, long after the wedding supper, Carrie changed into shorts and a sleeveless blouse. She sat on her front porch steps to catch the cool breeze of the evening. It had been a sweltering day, even for June, and since the church wasn't air-conditioned, everyone had left the wedding feeling a bit wilted.

The unnerving thought that she might actually faint during the ceremony had left Carrie with a tight, terrified sensation in her chest. She felt even worse when Greg gave her a friendly kiss after the reception and thanked her for all her help. The ache of loss had dulled only slightly since the afternoon.

Now, Carrie stretched her legs out and savored the coolness of the concrete against her bare skin. She could sit here all night, alone with her thoughts, letting the night air refresh her. But the screen door swung open suddenly and her father stepped outside. "Mind some company?" he asked.

"No, Dad," Carrie replied, not quite truthfully. She preferred being alone now, but she wouldn't hurt her father for the world.

He sat down beside her and breathed deeply. "Air feels good." They were silent for a minute before he added, "It was a beautiful wedding, wasn't it?"

"Yes," said Carrie softly. "I've never seen Kara look happier."

"And Greg?"

"Greg too," she admitted.

"I know it wasn't easy for you, honey."

She cast a sidelong glance at her father. "It was okay, Dad, really."

"If you say so."

"I do. Kara and Greg have their life, I have mine."

"What are your plans?"

"My plans?" repeated Carrie.

"You haven't talked about the fall. Are you returning to college?"

Carrie shrugged. "I don't know. Mother wants me to go back."

"You've already crammed three years into two. In another year you'll graduate. Then what?"

"I don't know."

"Haven't you thought about what you want to do?"

"I want to write," said Carrie wistfully. "I want to write a novel."

"All right," said Wilson, nodding. "You have the talent. What's stopping you?"

Carrie extended her hands in a gesture of futility. "Everything. This place, the pressures of college, the people and places I see every day."

Her father gave her a scrutinizing glance. "What are you saying, Carrie?"

"I'm not sure, Dad." She slowly shook her head. "I wasn't going to get into this—not now, not with you. I can't deal with it tonight."

"I don't understand, sweetheart."

Carrie bit her lip to keep from crying. "I don't want to go back to college, Daddy. I don't want to do anything. I feel as if I can't move or think straight or make decisions. I feel dead inside."

"Because of Greg?"

"Yes, Dad. It makes me feel guilty . . . Kara's my very own sister. Why can't I be happy for her? Why can't I forget Greg?"

Wilson put a sympathetic arm around Carrie's shoulder. "I'm sorry, baby," he murmured. "I had no idea it was this bad."

"I can't stay here in this town and pretend everything is fine," Carrie rushed on shakily. "I can't face Greg and Kara day after day. It was bad enough *before* they were married—"

"What do you want to do?"

"I don't know, Dad." She trembled slightly. "I'm twenty years old and I feel as if my life is falling apart."

"What about your faith, honey? Won't that hold you together?"

Carrie half smiled. "That sounds funny coming from you, Daddy."

He shrugged self-consciously. "Well, I've never understood it, but it's always been important to you and your mother."

"It still is, but right now . . ." Her voice trailed off.

"Well, then, why don't you go somewhere, get a fresh perspective on things?"

"Go where?"

"There must be some place where you could relax and sort things out for yourself, do some writing . . ."

"I don't have money for a vacation."

"I'll take care of the expense."

Carrie's voice was suddenly firm. "No, Dad. I couldn't let you do that."

"Then maybe you could find yourself a job."

"But then how could I write?"

Wilson was silent for a moment. Then he brightened. "I have an idea, Carrie. It's just a possibility, of course, but I was talking with a friend of mine, Woody Garrett, the other day. He runs a little art gallery up north near Madison, and he has a new artist— a talented craftsman. The man is a widower, new in the area, and he has a couple of kids who need looking after while he's out painting."

Carrie was perplexed. "You want me to be a baby-sitter?"

"Not exactly," said Wilson. "The man needs a live-in housekeeper, someone to be there with the children while he's on the road for weeks at a time. I guess he does paintings of people and landscapes in different areas. Maybe you could get a change of scene, earn a living, and still find some time to write."

"I don't know, Dad. The idea of working for some strange man and taking care of his children . . ."

"But you'd rarely see the man, and Woody says the children are easy to handle."

"What does Woody know about it?"

"Well, it's worth a try. It would be a chance to get away. Woody would handle the whole arrangement . . . and he could keep an eye on you for me," Wilson added with a chuckle.

"But what about college?"

"You could try the job just for the summer. By September I hope you'll have things worked out personally and be ready to tackle your studies again."

"I do love children," said Carrie tentatively.

"Woody placed an ad with me in today's paper for the position, but if we called him first thing in the morning—"

Carrie placed her hand on her father's. "Wait, Dad, please. Don't rush me. I need time to think."

"Sure, honey." Wilson ground his jaw lightly. "Maybe it's not really a good idea. But whatever you do, just don't waste your life moping around for a man you can never have. I've seen what that can do to a person—"

"You're talking about Kara's natural mother, aren't you?"

Wilson nodded, averting his eyes. "I'll never really get over it, Carrie. I didn't know how Kate felt about me, and I never guessed about the baby—about Kara. Catherine carried so much pain for so many years—" His voice broke. "I don't want that kind of pain for you, baby."

"I don't either, Daddy." Carrie's voice trembled. "I don't want to love Greg, Dad. I really don't want to." She was struggling to keep back the tears, but as quickly as she swallowed a sob, another one tore at her throat. "Why can't I stop loving him, Dad?"

Wilson embraced her tenderly. "Because you have always loved so fully. Go ahead and cry, honey. Believe me, you'll feel better."

Tears came in a torrent as Carrie sank into her father's arms. "When will it stop hurting?" she asked imploringly. "When will the ache go away?"

"In time," replied Wilson gently. "Maybe not today, or to-morrow, but someday. I promise you, Carrie, someday the hurt will be gone."

"Never gone, Daddy. I just pray that someday the hurt will be bearable."

Chapter Three

Two weeks passed. Carrie puttered aimlessly about the house, cleaned closets, worked in the garden, and read stacks of gothic novels from the library. She found one excuse after another to avoid making a decision about the position offered by Woody Garrett.

Finally, one evening at dinner, Wilson told her, "I talked with Woody today. That artist of his is still looking for someone to care for his children."

"Really?" she said without interest.

"He's had a string of temporary helpers, but if he doesn't find somebody permanent soon, he may have to give up his painting."

"Can't he paint at home?" inquired Lynn.

"He does area studies," replied Wilson. "I guess he has to go where the people and the scenery are."

"Well, I don't know that I want Carrie going so far away and staying in some strange house by herself."

"Oh, Mom, it's not that far," said Carrie. "Maybe six hours driving. And I'm not a child anymore. Lots of girls my age are married and have homes of their own."

"That's different," said Lynn. "You'd be alone with two children to care for. I'd rather you had a more conventional job."

"A regular job would keep me too tired to write."

"But you're not writing now," noted Lynn soberly, "and look at all the time on your hands."

Carried stared down at her plate. "I want to write . . . but I can't. I try . . . but nothing happens."

"That's why you need a change of scene," said Wilson. He smiled curiously. "You sound as if you might actually be considering Woody's offer."

"Maybe. I—I've thought about it."

"Woody's pulling for you, Carrie. He knows you're someone he could trust."

"I am good with kids . . . and I could write while they're sleeping or playing. I'd feel almost like . . . someone else. I'd be free of—of everything here."

"You could try it for a few weeks," suggested Wilson. "See how you like it."

Carrie stood up from the table. Her voice was more buoyant than it had been in weeks. "Do you have Woody's phone number, Dad? I'd like to give him a call."

Three days later, Carrie had her bags packed. Her father drove her to the bus depot, insisting all the while that he would have been glad to drive her to Madison.

"No, Dad," said Carrie with conviction. "It would have been a twelve-hour drive for you, round trip. I've got to do this on my own, right from the beginning."

"Well, Woody will meet you at the Madison depot. You remember him, don't you, hon—a thin-faced guy with friendly eyes and a wide mouth with spaces between his teeth?"

"When he smiles, his whole face crinkles," laughed Carrie.

"That's Woody," grinned Wilson. "He was a good buddy of mine back in college. He'd do anything for a friend. If you need help, he'll be there for you."

At dusk that evening, Sherwood Garrett greeted Carrie at the quaint, red-brick bus depot. He collected her baggage and escorted her to his large, late model station wagon.

"Last time I saw you, you were a little girl with braids and braces," he told her as he pulled onto the highway.

"You haven't changed at all, Mr. Garrett."

"Woody."

"Okay. Woody." Carrie glanced out the window. "How far is the house?"

"About six miles outside of Madison. It's a pleasant little trip—winding country roads."

"I thought the house was in town," said Carrie with concern. "How will I get around without a car?"

"Oh, Mr. Hawthorne took care of that. He left a car at the house for you. It's an old clunker, I'm afraid, but it'll get you into town and back."

"I didn't get to see much of Madison just now."

Woody flashed one of his smiles. "It's a typical small town where everyone knows everybody else's business. It's got what you need, but none of the frills of the city."

"I think I'll like it just fine," mused Carrie. They rode in amiable silence for several minutes. Then Carrie asked, "What can you tell me about my new employer?"

"Well," responded Woody, "his name is Nathan Hawthorne. He's one of the best painters I've seen, and someday he'll be famous."

"That's quite a recommendation," admitted Carrie. "How did you meet him?"

"One day about six months ago he walked into my gallery with a bunch of paintings under his arm." Woody's voice grew animated. "He was a quiet sort of man, but he asked me if I'd like to display his work and act as his agent. I took one look at his paintings and said yes. I've placed his work all over the country and made some big commissions. I never dreamed I'd represent such a fine artist. Heaven knows why he picked me to represent him in a backward little place like Madison, but I thank God he did."

Carrie smiled. "Now don't underrate yourself, Woody. My father says your gallery has a fine reputation among art critics."

"Well, I handle only top quality artists, I'll say that."

"Could you tell me more about Mr. Hawthorne? What's he like personally?" questioned Carrie.

Woody grew thoughtful. "I really don't know what to tell you. I've only seen the man a few times when he brought in a new supply of paintings. He's a loner, doesn't talk much. But he's very polite, refined.''

''What about his children?''

''He brought them in with him one time—a boy and a girl, about six and four, as I recall. Real well-behaved little kids. Some woman hired temporarily through the employment agency is staying with them until you get there.''

Ten minutes later Woody drove his station wagon up a winding, rutted driveway and stopped. Beyond a sprawling yard of overgrown grass sat a two-story house badly in need of paint and repair. Carrie managed to swallow her gasp as she stared at the ramshackle home.

But Woody emitted a long, low whistle. ''I hadn't seen the place till now,'' he told Carrie. ''It's not exactly what I had in mind.''

In the twilight, the house looked ominous. There were no other homes nearby, nothing on the landscape except several towering oaks with gnarled, twisting branches. ''It looks like something out of *Wuthering Heights*,'' murmured Carrie.

''I suppose this is all Mr. Hawthorne could find to rent, what with homes being in such short supply these days,'' observed Woody.

''It's probably very nice inside,'' added Carrie with a note of hope. Woody helped her out of the car and up the steep steps to the wide, sagging front porch. She waited with expectancy and trepidation as he knocked briskly on the door.

''Carrie, if you don't want to stay, just give the word. I'll drive you straight back to the depot.''

She laughed nervously. ''I'm sure that won't be necessary.''

The door opened. A rotund woman with steel-gray eyes and a broad, doughy face stared suspiciously at them.

''Hello,'' said Woody. ''I'm Sherwood Garrett. I called you earlier today. And this is Carrie Seyers, Mr. Hawthorne's new housekeeper.''

''It's about time!'' snapped the woman as she ushered them inside. ''I was hoping to get home before dark.''

''I had a long bus trip from Claremont,'' explained Carrie, her voice sounding more apologetic than she felt. She was tired and this rude woman sparked an immediate irritation.

The woman looked at Woody. "I'll fetch the children. Then I hope you can drive me back with you to Madison, Mr. Garrett."

He nodded.

"Good. Cabs cost an arm and a leg these days." The woman turned and called shrilly, "Dusty! Mindy! Get in here, you two!"

Within moments the youngsters entered the room with a dutiful formality. They stopped abruptly when they spotted Carrie and Woody. The boy was taller and older than the girl. He had dark, soulful eyes and wavy brown hair that covered his ears. The girl was small and delicate with blond curls and full, pink cheeks.

"Say hello to the nice people," prodded the large woman as she pinched their shoulders. Both children remained silent.

"Maybe you can drum some manners into them," the woman told Carrie impatiently. She looked down at the children. "Get yourselves to bed—pronto. Miss Seyers will be checking up on you."

"Yes, Miss Foggerty," replied the boy. The two scampered off immediately.

"They've had their dinner and their baths," the woman continued, "so you can relax tonight. Mr. Hawthorne left a whole list of instructions on the buffet. And he calls at least once a week to check on things. He's sure picky for being an absentee father."

"Which room is mine?" inquired Carrie uncertainly.

Miss Foggerty gestured expansively. "Take your pick. The room on the left upstairs has the most comfortable bed." She leaned conspiratorially toward Carrie. "If you want the truth, the whole place gives me the willies. Something's wrong here. I can't put my finger on it, but there's more here than meets the eye. Watch your step, young lady."

The woman picked up two suitcases and started for the door. "You ready, Mr. Garrett?"

Woody looked questioningly at Carrie.

"It's okay, Woody," she assured him. "Just bring in my luggage. I'll be fine."

"You sure?" he challenged.

Carrie nodded.

She was nodding again—and waving good-bye—ten minutes later when Woody pulled away with his new passenger, Miss Foggerty. Carrie stared through the darkness until the automobile lights were no longer visible on the winding driveway.

Then she went inside, locked the front door behind her, and stood alone in the silent, sparsely furnished house, shivering. Not from the cold, but from fright—and from a chilling sense of desolation. She wanted desperately to run after Woody and tell him she had to go home. She had made a dreadful mistake. She didn't belong here. Tears brimmed her eyes as she thought of her parents and brother at home in Claremont having a pleasant meal and enjoying one another's company.

"Oh, God, please help me," she whispered urgently. "Help me not to be afraid."

She stopped praying when she heard a sound from upstairs—a high, pitiable cry. "Mama—Mama!"

With an unexpected burst of energy, Carrie hurried upstairs toward the plaintive sounds. "I'm coming, children," she called. "Don't cry. I'll be right there!"

Chapter Four

Carrie peered uncertainly into the dark bedroom. The room was stuffy and smelled of musty furniture and yellowed wallpaper. "Children?" she said tentatively. "Are you okay?"

The boy said, "It's Mindy. She always cries."

Carrie entered the room and turned on a small table lamp. The children were in twin beds curled under several layers of comforters and quilts. The room looked as it smelled—ancient and unattended.

"Goodness, it's too warm for so many blankets," Carrie said, gently removing the covers from the little girl's shoulders. The child tugged the comforters back in place and covered her head.

"She don't like strangers," muttered her brother, sitting up.

Carrie sat down at the foot of his bed. "I'm sorry," she said softly. "We really weren't properly introduced, were we?"

"Miss Foggerty wanted to go home," said the boy. "Every day she wanted to go home, but she had to stay with us."

"Well, now I'm staying with you, and I don't want to go home," Carrie said brightly, consciously putting a cheerful tone into her voice.

"Will you stay until my daddy comes home?" questioned the boy.

"I suppose. When is he coming home?"

"I don't know."

"Well, until he does, I hope the three of us can have a good time together." Carrie looked over at the girl. The blankets had come down so that just her eyes showed.

Carrie reached out her hand to the boy. "I'm Carrie. And you're—?"

"Dusty. And my sister's Mindy. I'm six. She's four. I talk a lot, but she don't say nothing."

Carrie looked again at the two wide, woeful eyes above the blanket. "But I heard her call mama just a minute ago."

"That's all she says," reported Dusty. "She's dumb. She don't never talk anymore, not since . . ." His words drifted off.

Carrie frowned. "Not since?"

Dusty's voice was matter-of-fact. "Not since our mother died."

"I'm sorry," said Carrie quietly.

"Somebody killed her," continued the boy, "and maybe they'll kill us too." He scrunched down under the covers again.

Carrie stood up. She felt herself shiver involuntarily. "You mustn't say such things, Dusty. No one's going to hurt you. I'm here, and I'm going to take good care of you." She walked over to the window. "You need some fresh air in here."

"No!" cried Dusty. "The boogeyman will get in!"

Carrie promptly placed a high-back chair in front of the open window. "Now if any old boogeyman tries this window, he'll get his neck caught in the chair."

Dusty smiled gleefully. "And I'll hit him with my baseball bat."

"Don't be too hard on him," laughed Carrie. She turned off the lamp. "Good night, children. I'll be just down the hall if you need me."

She found the room Miss Foggerty had claimed had the best bed. It was large and lumpy, but it would do. As she dressed for bed, she couldn't shake the terrible sense of aloneness she felt. She wondered why anybody in his right mind would bring two young, impressionable children to a place like this to live, so far from the rest of the world. Somehow it seemed a million miles from everything that was warm and familiar. Carrie had tried her best to comfort the children, but who, she wondered now, would comfort her?

In the privacy of her room she spoke out loud. "Jesus, I don't like it here. I feel alone—and a little scared. I want to leave. But the children . . .'' Carrie thought of their watchful eyes, about Mindy's refusal to speak. "They need someone to care for them. Help me be braver than I feel!''

Talking with God somehow made the old house seem less depressing. With a slight smile Carrie added, "And you know how much I want to write. Help me with that, too.''

There was more to Carrie's prayer, but sleep washed away the words.

Dusty was the first one up in the morning. He came running into Carrie's room and scrambled up on the bed. "It did it, Carrie,'' he exulted. "It kept him out!''

Carrie looked up groggily. "What? Who?''

"The chair,'' persisted the boy. "The chair kept out the boogeyman!''

"That's wonderful,'' she mumbled. Her mouth was dry and tasted like glue. She reached for her robe and pulled it around her. If only she could make it to the kitchen to get some coffee or juice, she'd know whether she was in fact dead or alive.

Dusty followed her, talking nonstop. It was too early for Carrie to focus on even the sanest of conversations, so she allowed his torrent of words to fly right on by. "What do you think, Carrie?'' he said at last, stopping to catch a much-needed breath.

"Think about what?'' she questioned as she turned a can of frozen orange juice under the running tap water.

"About going hiking. Miss Foggerty said there are wolves in the woods. We could catch a baby one for a pet.''

"A wolf for a pet?'' gasped Carrie.

"I used to have a dog,'' said Dusty wistfully. "A collie like Lassie. His name was Mr. T. But when Daddy took us, he didn't take my dog.''

"Took you?'' Carrie repeated, puzzled. "What do you mean?''

"Nothing.'' Dusty looked away quickly. "I'll wake up Mindy,'' he said. "She's sleeping all day.''

"No, Dusty,'' Carrie called after him. "It's only 6:30.'' But he was already taking the stairs two at a time.

After breakfast, Carrie explored the house, with Dusty eager to act as a tour guide and Mindy silently following a few steps behind. Some of the rooms were empty; others contained only rudimentary furnishings—a sofa, a table, a chair or two. The furniture was old and faded, the sofas overstuffed and spewing tufts of cotton from ruptured seams.

"What do you do all day?" Carrie asked as she and the children returned to the kitchen.

"We play," replied Dusty. "And Daddy brought us a TV last time he came. I watch Plastic Man and Popeye and Smurfs on Saturday."

"I see," said Carrie. "Do you ever study, you know, like in school?"

"Naw," scoffed Dusty. He thought a moment. "I went to kindergarten when we lived at Grandma's, but I had to go away before the Christmas party."

"Why did you go away?"

"Daddy came for us. I didn't get my Christmas tree. I made it myself. It's still at school."

"You didn't get to finish kindergarten?"

Dusty shook his head, then walked over to the cookie jar. "Can I have one? I'm hungry."

"It's nearly empty," observed Carrie. "In fact, the cupboards are bare too. We'd better drive into town and stock up on groceries."

"But Daddy never takes us to town," said Dusty.

"Well, I do," Carrie replied. She paused as a startling realization struck her. "I didn't think to ask about money."

Smiling knowingly, Dusty brought Carrie his father's list of instructions. Aloud she read, "Pick up household spending money each Tuesday at post office box 6208." Carrie sighed with relief. "Come on, kids, it's Tuesday. Let's go find Box 6208."

Chapter Five

The summer days fell into a pleasant pattern for Carrie and the children. Each morning the youngsters awoke early and did their chores—made their beds, put away their pajamas, and helped set the table for breakfast—while Carrie made breakfast.

Carrie had the house gleaming now, as much as a tired old house could gleam. Almost every day the children made a dazzling painting with huge brushes and large jars of poster paint. Then they hung their posterboard creations all over the house so that each room boasted an original—and often startling—splash of color.

After lunch the children studied. Carrie had purchased coloring books and checked out dozens of books from the Madison library—beginning readers, ABC books, and simple juvenile adventure novels. She also bought a Bible storybook and read to the children about David and Goliath, Peter and Paul, and of course, Jesus. The children were always attentive and seemed eager to learn. Even Mindy seemed to enjoy it, although she still refused to speak.

Often in the afternoons, Carrie and the children took walks in the adjoining woods, picking wild flowers and collecting samples of leaves to wax and press in a book. Except for Wednesday evenings when Nathan Hawthorne made his usual eight p.m. call, Carrie always gave the children an early dinner and had them in bed by seven. That gave her the rest of the evening to work on her novel.

Carrie found that the change of scene and her new lifestyle

were conducive to writing. The words flowed for the first time in many months. Each week she completed two or three chapters. Her confidence blossomed; she could sense her work taking on a richness and depth it previously lacked. Daily she thanked the Lord for bringing her to this strange old house and to the two children she had already grown to love. She was grateful, too, for the reassuring phone calls from Woody and the frequent, encouraging letters from her parents. Except for those buried, persistent yearnings for Greg, her days were warm and promising.

Only the nights presented a problem for Carrie. In the dark, the house took on sinister proportions. It creaked and rattled; the wind whistled through broken eaves and capriciously banged loose shutters. Carrie found herself repeatedly succumbing to the unwelcome ache of facing the long nights alone. She seriously doubted that she would have stayed, even for the children, if she hadn't known that somehow God was there, caring for her, protecting her, and giving her enough courage. It didn't help to be awakened night after night out of a dead sleep by Mindy's terrified screams. The child who maintained absolute silence by day vented her deep terror at night.

Carrie always rushed into the children's room and gathered the trembling youngster into her arms. Mindy's cry was always the same: "Mama . . . Mama. . . !"

"There, there, baby," Carrie would whisper. "We all love you. Dusty loves you. I love you. Jesus loves you." Eventually Mindy's body would relax again in sleep and Carrie would gently tuck her back in bed. But inevitably, it seemed to Carrie, all of the child's tension had been absorbed by her own body, and she realized with her usual dismay that sleep would be elusive for an hour or two.

During those sleepless hours, night following night, Carrie wondered about the children and their parents. What terrible thing had happened to their mother to elicit such nightmares in Mindy? How had the woman died? The children had implied some unspeakable tragedy. But what? And what about their father? He telephoned regularly and sent original, handpainted postcards the children adored, but why did he stay away for weeks—even months—at a time, especially now when the children's grief over their mother's death was so fresh? What kind of cruel, insensitive man was he to pawn off his parental responsibility on a stranger? And what if he had secured someone less conscientious or dependable than Carrie to care for them? Carrie shuddered to think of the awful possibilities.

One afternoon following the children's lessons, Carrie decided to try to coax Mindy to speak. She reasoned that if the girl regained her normal verbal expression, the nightmares might cease. So, looking the child in the eye, Carrie said firmly but kindly, "What is your name? Can you say your name?"

Mindy stared back, unblinking.

Carrie persisted. "Can you say, 'My name is Mindy Hawthorne'?"

The child shook her head.

"Please," said Carrie urgently. "Just once. 'My name is Mindy Hawthorne.' "

The child twisted her mouth slightly and announced with defiance, "My name is Mindy Havers."

Carrie stared at her with a mixture of astonishment and perplexity. "That's wonderful, Mindy!" she exclaimed. "But you mean Hawthorne. Mindy Hawthorne."

"Mindy Havers," the child said again.

Dusty scrambled over to his sister and looked her full in the face. "It's Hawthorne, Mindy," he said emphatically. "Remember what Daddy said?"

Mindy made a face, turned, and ran out the door. Dusty looked sheepishly at Carrie. "She's just a baby. She gets mixed up sometimes."

"Well, at least we've made progress," said Carrie. "She finally said something besides 'Mama.' Maybe tonight there won't be any nightmares."

But that evening was marked by something else—an extraordinary, unexpected event. Carrie had just put the children to bed when there was an abrupt knock at the door. Her heart lurched. They never had visitors, especially not at night. Carrie cautiously approached the door and called out, "Who's there?"

A familiar deep voice replied, ''Nathan Hawthorne.''

Carrie hesitated. Was it possible? The man hadn't shown his face at the house all summer. Why now, without warning, and at night?

''How can I be sure it's you?'' she asked.

There was a pause, then the voice recited, ''I'm a wandering artist with two bright, beautiful children. Dusty is six, Mindy is four. And I'm pleased to see that my friend Sherwood Garrett hired such a cautious, capable housekeeper, whom I speak with every Wednesday at eight.''

Carrie, surmising that only the real Mr. Hawthorne would have such facts at his fingertips, swung open the door with relief. She looked up then into the face of one of the most disarming individuals she had ever seen. The man stood over six feet tall, had dark brown hair and brows, a sun-bronzed complexion, and strong, chisled features. His jaw was solid, his nose straight, his mouth full and sensitively drawn.

Carrie blushed as she realized how intently she was staring.

''You must be Miss Seyers,'' he observed with a smile. ''May I come in?''

''Oh, of course,'' she replied, flustered. She stepped aside. ''I—we weren't expecting you. I'm sorry.''

The man waved off her apology. ''I'm the one who's sorry. I should have telephoned instead of just popping in like this.''

Carrie asked honestly, ''Why didn't you?''

He shrugged. ''I just decided it was time to come home. I'm afraid I'm rather impetuous—and a bit thoughtless at times. I hope you won't hold it against me.'' He removed his worn leather jacket and cast it over a chair. ''How are the children?''

''They're fine,'' replied Carrie. ''Mindy even said her name today.''

''Wonderful!'' exclaimed Nathan. ''Her silence has been one of my main concerns.'' He looked around. ''Where are they?''

''They're upstairs asleep.''

''I won't wake them. I'll just take a peek.''

But before Nathan could ascend the stairs, his two children came bounding down the steps, shouting with glee. Even silent little Mindy was crying, "Daddy . . . Daddy!"

Carrie felt a rush of warmth inside as she watched the huge man kneel and tenderly gather the youngsters into his arms. Their eager arms circled his neck as they smothered his cheeks with kisses, each trying to outdo the other.

"Okay, okay," he said, laughing. "Let a fellow get some air!" He set them down and steered them over to Carrie. "Aren't they the best kids you ever saw, Miss Seyers?"

"They certainly are," she agreed sincerely.

He stooped down again before the children, his eyes twinkling, and said, "What shall we do to celebrate my homecoming?"

"We could have hot chocolate and cookies," suggested Dusty.

Nathan straightened up and waved his arms expansively. "Hot chocolate and cookies it is!" Then glancing at Carrie, he added, "If Miss Seyers agrees."

"I—I guess so. Come along. I'll fix it."

They headed for the kitchen, Carrie feeling a bit overwhelmed, while the youngsters energetically pulled their father along, each tugging an arm.

Carrie warmed the chocolate milk while Dusty and Mindy showed their father their bright, bold paintings that graced every wall, and their Play-doh figures and egg-carton flowers.

"You children are certainly developing your artistic abilities," marveled Nathan. He looked over at Carrie. "You've been working with them, haven't you, Miss Seyers?"

Carrie felt her face flush. She looked down at the pan of hot chocolate. "They have your natural ability, Mr. Hawthorne." She added shyly, "I'm looking forward to seeing some of your work."

"I have several paintings out in my van. I'll show them to you in the morning."

"That would be very nice, Mr. Hawthorne."

"Call me Nathan, please."

"All right. Nathan—if you'll call me Carrie."

He grinned—the most compelling smile she'd ever seen. "You have a deal . . . Carrie."

Chapter Six

If Carrie assumed that Nathan Hawthorne was an exuberant, outgoing man, she realized quickly how mistaken she was. After the children were tucked back into bed, she literally saw the change creep across his face. Almost immediately his mood switched from jovial to somber. Carrie felt disappointed. Evidently Nathan had put on a buoyant, cheerful facade just for the sake of his children.

Now, where the laugh lines had been, anxious furrows sank into place. For nearly ten minutes Nathan paced about the house checking windows and doors. He thumbed nervously through the mail that had accumulated during his absence—mostly advertising circulars and an occasional bill. Carrie had already noticed that no personal mail ever arrived for Nathan Hawthorne.

"Is this all there is?" he asked her crisply, holding up the ads and bills.

"Yes. Except for the letters that come for me from my family and friends."

"Has anyone been here looking for me?"

Carrie shook her head, puzzled. "No. Are you expecting someone?"

He turned away abruptly and dismissed her inquiry with a vague, "I thought perhaps a client might have stopped by."

"Your agent Woody Garrett telephones once in a while to see how things are, but no, there's been no one here at the house. In fact, it gets rather lonely around here at times."

He pivoted and raised one eyebrow as he queried, "Are you saying you're unhappy here?"

"No, not at all," said Carrie quickly. "I love the children, and I've been able to get quite a bit done on my novel."

Nathan's briskness gave way to fleeting curiosity. "A novel? Are you a writer?"

She flushed slightly. "I'm trying to be. I haven't published anything yet."

"Do you write just fiction?" he asked, his words precise.

"Yes, that's my main interest."

"Well," he said, his voice growing pleasant, "one of these days we'll have to sit down and talk about your novel."

"I—I'd love to. And I'd like to hear all about your work, Mr. Hawthorne. Woody is very impressed by your talent."

"We'll talk tomorrow," Nathan told her. "Right now I'm very tired. I drove a long distance today. So if you'll excuse me, I'll go on up to my room."

Carrie raised her hand in alarm. "Oh, I hope I haven't already taken your room, Mr. Hawthorne."

"Nathan," he corrected. "And if you have, it doesn't matter. I'm not fussy. I'll sleep anywhere. Just give me a freshly made bed."

"Well, I'm afraid I took the most comfortable bed. You see, the former housekeeper suggested—"

"It's all right, Carrie. Just get me some sheets. I'll take care of myself."

"How—how long will you be staying?"

"I don't know. A day . . . a week . . . until it's time to go again."

That night Carrie found it hard to sleep. The excitement of the evening still tensed her muscles, and through her mind ran the opposing images of Nathan Hawthorne—the affectionate, cheerful father and the somber, almost brusque man. Why had he come home so suddenly, without warning, at such an hour? How would everyday life change now that he was here? She had known he would show up someday, but she hadn't counted on him being such an unsettling individual—somehow fascinating and forbidding at once.

Some time in the early morning, after several hours of restless slumber, Carrie awoke, startled. She heard something downstairs. Had someone broken in? Quietly she rose and stole to the head of the stairs. She descended a few steps, then peered down into the shadows of the living room. There at the desk by the front window sat Nathan Hawthorne, his muscular frame outlined by the first wash of dawn, his elbows squarely on the desk, his head in his hands. Was he weeping? Praying? Grieving? Something in the way he sat gave the impression of profound desolation. Carrie, embarrassed to have stumbled upon so private and painful a moment, turned away and hurried back to her room.

At breakfast, to Carrie's bewilderment, Nathan seemed carefree once more. He bounced the children on his knee, swung them in the air, and listened raptly as they recounted their adventures of the past six weeks.

After breakfast, at Carrie's prompting, the children reluctantly left their father's side and went out to play. Nathan sat leisurely drinking his coffee and appeared in a receptive frame of mind. As Carrie cleared the table, she decided now would be as good a time as any to bring up some household problems that had been on her mind. "There are some things that need to be done around here," she began. "Perhaps now that you're home, you could tell me what to do about them."

"What things?" inquired Nathan.

"The washing machine isn't working well. I'd like to have someone come out and fix it."

"I'll take a look at it myself," he replied. "What else?"

"Well, the children need more clothes. They wear the same things over and over. I thought you might want to take them into town shopping. I know they'd enjoy it."

"No," said Nathan sharply. "I'll give you some extra money. You go buy them what they need."

"Well, I'll go along, of course," said Carrie, "but I thought you might like to pick out some things for them yourself."

"I'll trust your judgment."

"All right." She hesitated. "It's nearly August, Mr. Haw-thorne—I mean, Nathan. I was wondering what I should do about registering Dusty for school in September."

"Do nothing," said Nathan briskly. "I want him here at home. You can teach him, can't you?"

"I'm hardly qualified," Carrie protested. "Besides, Dusty needs to be in school with others his age. We live so far out that he and Mindy have no friends, no one to play with."

"They have you. I pay you to take care of them and to keep them happy."

"I do my best," Carrie said softly.

Nathan smiled. "Yes, I can see that you do." He reached into his wallet and withdrew several large bills. "Here, Carrie, you go shopping, and the children and I will work on that old clunker of a washing machine."

Carrie stared at him, bewildered. "But, Nathan, the children have to go with me to try on their clothes."

"No, they don't. You know their sizes."

"But they need to get out of this house. They always love going to town to shop."

He grimaced. "Do you take them to town often?"

"Every time I go. I certainly wouldn't leave them here alone."

"Then take them," he said, his teeth clenched. He swung around and stalked out of the kitchen without another word.

"Come, children," Carrie called out the door, deciding to delay trying to figure out Nathan's strange attitudes. "Let's get ready to go shopping!"

The children were excited about the prospect of buying new clothes. As Carrie drove them into Madison, Dusty talked incessantly about what they would get. Even Mindy joined in with an eager word or two.

"I want clothes just like I left at Grandma's," Dusty said earnestly.

"You left your clothes at your grandmother's?" questioned Carrie. "Where does she live?"

"Far away," replied Dusty.

Carrie was intrigued. "Why didn't you bring your clothes with you?"

"We couldn't," said Dusty practically. "Daddy came for us when it was dark. He didn't want to wake up Grandma."

"You mean you left your grandmother's without saying good-bye?"

"Daddy said we had to be quiet. He said we were playing a game—like hide-and-go-seek."

"You mean your grandmother doesn't know where you are?"

Carrie caught Dusty's mischievous smile in the rearview mirror.

"No, she hasn't found us yet," he said. He looked momentarily thoughtful, then pushed out his lower lip. "I wish she'd hurry up though. Grandma's got all our good toys."

For Carrie, the joy of their shopping trip was dampened by new, troubling thoughts. She began to put together pieces—innocent remarks the children had made, Nathan's behavior—and what she came up with was more than a little disturbing.

Apparently Nathan Hawthorne had taken his children from the grandparents' home without their knowledge. What reason would he have? Why were the children living with their grandparents in the first place? What really happened to Nathan's wife? Was she dead as the children believed? Or was it possible that Nathan had stolen the children from their mother and was actually deceiving them about her death? That sort of thing happened these days, especially among divorced families. Perhaps the poor woman was even now searching desperately for her babies. The idea was shattering. It couldn't be!

But one fact was distressingly clear. Nathan Hawthorne was hiding something.

Chapter Seven

On Sunday Carrie pushed her nagging questions about Nathan Hawthorne to the back of her mind. She rose early, bathed and dressed, then roused the children. While they scrambled eagerly into new outfits, she went downstairs to prepare breakfast.

Nathan entered the kitchen moments later, his hair still rumpled from sleep. "What's all the commotion so early in the morning?" he demanded of Carrie.

She looked at him abashed. "I'm so sorry we woke you, Mr. Haw—Nathan. The children and I are going to church." She felt herself rushing nervously to get the words out. "I should have asked you last night if you'd like to join us."

"What church—that little chapel in Madison?"

"Yes. The children enjoy it so much. Would you like to come?"

"No!" he snapped. "And I see no reason for the children to go."

"Oh, but they'll be so disappointed. I've taken them every Sunday."

Nathan's eyes narrowed; then he waved his hand abruptly. "All right, go ahead." Thoughtfully he added, "Their mother used to take them to church too . . ."

"We'll be back by noon," she assured him.

"If you don't get stuck with a long-winded preacher," he grunted.

In fact, Carrie and the youngsters were back home several

minutes before noon, and much to Carrie's surprise, Nathan was whistling in the kitchen as he made tuna-fish sandwiches.

"I thought we'd go on a picnic," he announced as she stared at him. "It'll save you cooking. Look, it's all packed—potato chips, pork and beans, bananas, lemonade—"

"Yippee!" exclaimed Dusty. Mindy gave her father a vigorous hug.

"Just give us a minute to change our clothes," said Carrie, finding her voice at last. "A picnic will be—wonderful!"

They hiked through the woods to a picturesque spot nearly a half-mile from the house. Carrie was winded, but Nathan, in top form, was not even mildly out of breath. Then, of course, he spent his days out of doors, hiking and painting. Naturally he would be physically fit.

Nathan found a smooth, grassy spot and spread out the blanket. Carrie unpacked the picnic basket, placing items on each corner to hold it in place from the breeze.

"Here come the ants," cheered Dusty, hunched down, his nose nearly pressed against the ground.

"Tell them they need a reservation," laughed Carrie.

The simple food tasted delicious in the warm summer air. After they had eaten their fill, Carrie sat back and relaxed, breathing deeply. She hadn't felt so good in weeks. She noticed that Nathan's expression was relaxed too. He looked almost happy. They watched the children chase each other from tree to tree and throw bread crumbs to the birds. The youngsters made ragged bouquets of wildflowers and weeds and pursued unsuspecting chipmunks and squirrels.

"I'm sure glad Mindy is talking again," Nathan remarked. "She seems almost like her old self now."

"I think it's because you're home," said Carrie.

"It's just as much because of you, Carrie. She responds to your loving care." Nathan helped himself to a banana and offered half to Carrie.

"No thanks," she said with a smile. "I'm stuffed."

He smiled back. "All right, while I'm stuffing myself, you tell me about your novel."

Carrie caught her breath. She couldn't help noticing that Nathan, when he wasn't so somber and stern, was an extraordinarily handsome man. "My novel?" she repeated. "Goodness, I don't know where to begin."

"How about the beginning?"

"Well, okay." Carrie spoke falteringly at first, telling Nathan about her romance novel with its New England setting. She told him how she had researched her material and developed her ideas. The more she spoke, the more confident she felt. She sensed that Nathan was genuinely interested and that he liked her idea. Yes, it was a good story. She believed that. And Nathan seemed to believe it too!

When she had finished speaking, he asked with a twinkle, "Is this love story autobiographical?"

She blushed and looked away momentarily. "Only in rather small parts," she admitted.

"I love good literature," Nathan remarked as he sat forward and circled his knees with his arms. "A person can paint beautiful pictures with words just as he can with a brush on canvas."

"Oh, I believe that too," said Carrie excitedly. "Look at the great poets—Edna St. Vincent Millay, Dylan Thomas, T. S. Elliot—"

"One of my favorites," interjected Nathan, "is Federico Garcia Lorca. He was a Spanish poet, so most Americans haven't heard of him. But his images are exquisite."

"I'd love to read some of his works," mused Carrie.

"I may have a book of his poems," said Nathan. "I'll check."

"How did you discover him?"

"In college. I minored in Spanish. But Lorca's work would appeal to anyone. He had a very earthy, colorful, lyrical style. For example, he talks about 'men whose bones ring out, who sing with mouths full of sun and flint.' "

"I like that," said Carrie thoughtfully.

"He was something of an artist too. He loved painting and was a good friend of Salvador Dali. Maybe it's the artist in me that likes him so well."

"Is he still living?" inquired Carrie.

Nathan's face sobered. "No. He died in 1936, at the beginning of the Civil War in Spain. He was taken out and senselessly shot, then thrown into an unmarked grave."

"How terrible!"

Nathan picked up a twig and snapped it between his fingers. He ground his jaw. "The good people of this world always die tragically," he muttered. Carrie wondered if he was still talking about the poet Lorca.

Their stimulating literary conversation faltered after that. Carrie could almost see Nathan closing in upon himself, shutting out the world—and her. Why did he swing between such extreme moods? What secret torments turned him from a responsive conversation-alist one moment into a morose stranger the next?

It was nearly dusk when the weary troupe of picnickers arrived home. After a light supper, Nathan carried the children up to their beds, and both he and Carrie helped the sleepy youngsters into their pajamas. After Nathan tucked them in, Carrie prayed briefly with the children, then kissed them good night.

"Is that a nightly ritual?" Nathan asked her when they were out in the hall.

"What?"

"The prayer and good-night kisses."

"The children feel safer when we pray—and I think every child should be kissed good night."

Nathan smiled relentingly. "So do I, Carrie." Somehow, his words seemed to go beyond the children. For an instant, Carrie had the startling impression that Nathan was thinking of kissing her!

"Well, then, if that's all," she said quickly, "good night, Mr. Hawthorne."

"Nathan."

"I mean Nathan."

"Good night, Carrie. Thank you for a delightful day."

It was early yet, but Carrie went straight to her room and shut the door behind her. The fresh air and exercise had made her pleasantly sleepy, so she relished the idea of a couple of hours of extra sleep. The thought of a warm bath was equally appealing, but the bathroom was down the hall next to Nathan's room. She decided to skip the bath.

Carrie was just about to turn out her light when there was a knock on the door. She opened the door a crack and peered out at Nathan Hawthorne.

"I'm sorry to bother you, Carrie," he said quietly, "but I found the volume of Lorca's poetry. I thought you might enjoy looking it over before you go to sleep tonight."

She pulled her robe more snugly around her, then opened the door and took the book. "Thank you, Nathan. That's very thoughtful of you." She hesitated as an idea occurred to her. "Would you wait a minute? I have a book for you too." She went to her desk and returned with a slim volume.

"What's this?" he asked, turning it over in his hands.

"My favorite poems," she told him. "*The Psalms of David.*"

"Oh, yes. From the Bible."

"Yes. Have you read them?"

"I gave them a dutiful glance in a college literature course years ago."

"Well, if you'll spend some time with them, I think you'll enjoy them. I have a feeling that in some ways you and David are very much alike."

Faint curiosity flickered in his eyes. "Really? Well, I'll let you know if you're right." He turned to go, then looked back with a wry smile, and said, "Pleasant reading, Carrie."

"You too, Nathan. You too."

Chapter Eight

The next morning, while the children played outside, Nathan and Carrie enjoyed a second cup of coffee. After several minutes of casual chitchat, he gave her a curious smile and asked, "What did you think of Lorca?"

"I loved him," Carrie replied eagerly. "His images are so colorful and rich, almost . . . sensual. I went to sleep with his expressions whirling in my mind."

"Really? Which ones?"

"Oh, let's see if I can remember. One was . . . 'August, counterpoints of sugar and peach.' Another was when he spoke of children eating 'brown bread and delicious moon.' "

"Those are from his poem, 'Agosto.' "

"Yes, but I was even more touched by a stanza from another of his poems. I don't recall the title, but I memorized the phrases."

"Tell me."

Slowly she recited:

Thus would I have you, familiar God.
Little flour wafer for the newborn child.
Wind and substance joined in exact expression.
By love for the flesh which knows not your name.

Nathan nodded. "That is one of Lorca's most haunting, unforgettable refrains."

"He's speaking about God, isn't he—and about man's relationship with Him?"

"I think he's speaking of the universal contradiction of man's desire to know God and his inability to do so."

"But that's so sad," reflected Carrie. "It doesn't have to be that way."

"Maybe not, but it usually is."

"I don't believe that. I mean, I know God never meant for it to be difficult for us to know Him. He created us to have fellowship with Him."

Nathan gazed curiously at her. "You mean you believe a person can actually know God as something more than a vague ideal?"

"Of course. When our sin separated us from God, He made it possible for us to know Him personally through His Son, Jesus Christ. Since Jesus took our punishment, God can accept us as His children."

"Well, now you're leaving the realm of philosophy for theology."

"No, it's all in the realm of truth. It's what the Bible teaches."

"And I suppose you believe the 'Good Book' from cover to cover?"

"I've staked my life on it," said Carrie simply.

Nathan grew thoughtful. "Well, I do have to admit I was impressed by those Psalms you gave me last night."

"Then you did read them?"

"Yes. I opened the book to Psalm 69. I read it over and over. I found myself fascinated by this David of yours."

"Really? What did you like about him?"

"I don't know if I can put it into words. The man seemed in such distress, in such agony of soul. He had enemies who pursued him and persecuted him without cause, yet he maintained such an unswerving trust in this God of his. He carried on such an intimate, earnest conversation with Him, as if God were his closest friend—"

"God does give consolation during times of trouble," interjected Carrie.

"Well, yes. If you believe in Him, I suppose your faith can be quite comforting."

"It's not one's faith that gives comfort; it's Jesus, the source of that faith."

"Well, I believe faith is faith, whatever the source—"

"Misplaced faith is pure foolishness," argued Carrie. "If you were drowning, you wouldn't want to place your faith in a leaky boat. You'd want a ship that could get you safely to shore."

Nathan rubbed his chin thoughtfully. "I don't know much about faith or about David's God," he said quietly, looking away. He appeared to be speaking almost to himself. "But I do know David the man. I understand how he felt when he said, 'Reproach hath broken my heart. . . . I am full of heaviness; and I looked for some to take pity, but there was none; and for comforters, but I found none.' "

Carrie looked closely at Nathan. "I'm sorry, I'm not sure I know what you mean."

He looked up, startled, and then smiled painfully. "Of course you don't, Carrie. And that's best, believe me."

He excused himself then and went directly to his room. A half hour later he came downstairs carrying his suitcase.

Carrie looked at him in surprise. "Are you leaving?"

He approached her until they stood just a foot apart, then gazed seriously into her face. His eyes were so penetrating she had to force her gaze to remain steady.

"I have to go," he told her.

"Why?"

"I have to paint. Remember, I've got two children to support." He smiled wryly. "Plus a very lovely housekeeper." He paused. "No, not just a housekeeper. A friend."

"Thank you," she said shyly. "When will you be back?"

"I don't know. A week . . . two . . ."

She managed a smile. "But what about the children? They're playing in the backyard."

His eyes held hers. "I know. I'll tell them good-bye outside. I'll miss you all."

"I'll finish Lorca while you're gone."

He patted his shirt pocket. "I've got your book of Psalms right here. It's going with me."

"I'm glad." She hesitated, then added, "I'll pray for you."

He grinned. "Thanks. I can use all the prayers you've got."

After Nathan left, the house felt disturbingly empty. Carrie was plagued by spells of loneliness. She wondered how one man's presence could have made such a difference. She sensed it everywhere—the tedious, solitary gloom surrounding the house, the hollow sound in the rooms, the lengthening shadows that ushered in the often restless nights.

But gradually Carrie and the children adjusted to being alone again. Within a few days they had returned to their "pre-Nathan" schedule—the children studying and playing and Carrie working each evening on her novel. There was only one noticeable difference—Carrie's fresh sense of yearning for adult companionship. Until Nathan, she had been satisfied to spend her days alone with the children; now she had to admit she needed more.

As if in answer to her unspoken longing, Carrie met Frank Colbin. He appeared at her door one day with a tentative smile on his earnest face and a painting tucked under his arm.

"May I help you?" she asked when she had opened the door halfway.

"I'm looking for someone," he said softly.

"Who?"

He coughed nervously, then proceeded in a rush of words. "The artist who did this painting." He held it up.

"Oh, yes, that's one of Nathan's works," she responded admiringly. "It's definitely his style."

"Yes, I thought so. The man who owns the gallery just outside of Madison, a man named Sherwood Garrett, told me Nathan Hawthorne painted it. He sent me here. He said I'd find the artist here."

"Well, he's not at home right now," said Carrie.

"Oh, he's away?" inquired the man, looking disconcerted.

"He spends a lot of time on the road painting."

"And you're his—his wife?"

Carrie laughed lightly. "No, I'm his housekeeper, and I take care of his children."

The man's delicately carved features shifted slightly and his eyes grew intent. "His children, you say? You care for his children?"

"Why, yes," replied Carrie, a bit perplexed by the peculiar direction of their conversation. "Is there some message I could give Mr. Hawthorne if he should telephone?"

The man ran his fingertips over the sparse hair on his forehead. "Forgive me, miss. I stupidly assumed you knew why I was here." He gestured toward the painting under his arm. "I want to commission Mr. Hawthorne to do a painting for me. I admire his exceptional talent, but the man's modesty is baffling. I've spent days trying to locate him, but no one in town seems to be acquainted with him, nor even to have heard of his remarkable abilities. And I practically had to bribe Mr. Garrett before he would relinquish Mr. Hawthorne's address." He muffled a nervous chuckle. "I don't mean bribe. That's just a joke."

"Well, Mr. Hawthorne is a very private man," admitted Carrie.

"Nothing wrong with that, I suppose," remarked the man, "unless, of course, someone has something to hide."

"If you'll give me your name and address," said Carrie, "I'll have Mr. Hawthorne get in touch with you on his return."

"That won't be necessary, miss. I'll be in touch with you again. I have a rather erratic schedule, you see. I'm in and out." He pointed down the road and asked, "Are you familiar with the old Norton house?"

Carrie nodded. "Yes, it's about a mile from here. I drive by it whenever I go into Madison."

"Well, I'm renting it now," he said, his words quick and breathy. He smiled and his face took on a certain fragile attractiveness. "I guess that makes us neighbors."

Carrie smiled back. "I guess it does."

He held out his hand. "I'm Frank Colbin."

"I'm Carrie Seyers," she replied, extending her hand. She noticed that for a man of slight stature, Frank's handshake was reassuringly firm.

Chapter Nine

The next day Carrie received a telephone call from Frank. "I don't mean this to sound forward, or like a line, Miss Seyers," he said hesitantly, "but I've been thinking about you. You were very kind to me yesterday, and I would like to show my appreciation."

"But I didn't do anything," protested Carrie.

"Oh, but you did. You were very patient with my bumbling inquiry about Mr. Hawthorne. Now, to make up for our rather awkward introduction, I would like very much to take you to dinner this evening."

"That's really not necessary, Mr. Colbin."

"Perhaps not, but I would greatly enjoy your company. If you wish, you could meet me at the restaurant and leave immediately afterward."

"Actually, I have other plans for tonight."

"Oh? A date?"

"No. I'm going to a Christian concert at the little chapel in Madison."

"Really? What a coincidence. I've been looking for a satisfactory church. Would you consider allowing me to escort you?"

Carrie caught her breath. "Then you're a Christian, Mr. Colbin?"

The man laughed delightedly. "And you, Miss Seyers? How fortunate we are to have found each other!"

"The concert begins at seven-thirty," she noted.

"Fine, then we still have time for dinner together."

"I—I suppose that would be all right."

"Are you familiar with the Fair Winds restaurant in Madison?"

"Yes, I've driven by it several times."

"Well, it's a nice place, not like most of the local beaneries," he remarked with a mild note of condescension. "I'll tell you what, Miss Seyers. I have a job interview at four this afternoon, but I could meet you at the restaurant at six."

"Goodness, I'll have to see if the baby-sitter can come any earlier."

"Please do try, Miss Seyers. There already seems to be a spiritual bond between us. I think we'll find mutual encouragement in being friends."

Carrie smiled in spite of herself. "You certainly have a way with words, Mr. Colbin. Very well. I'll call the sitter now. And I'll see you at the restaurant at six."

Carrie hung up the receiver feeling a bit dazed. Had she actually just accepted an invitation for a date with an intriguing stranger? Certainly she never would have behaved quite so daringly at home. But hadn't Frank said he was a Christian? Maybe he was God's answer to her loneliness.

Dusty was watching her curiously. "You look funny, Carrie," he said.

She looked at him. "Oh, goodness, Dusty, I've got to call Miss Foggerty and see if she can come early tonight."

"Miss Foggerty?" he repeated, the last syllable arching shrilly. "Oh, yuk!"

Carrie laughed, then chided, "Now, Dusty, a dose of Miss Foggerty once in a while won't hurt anyone."

"But it won't help none, either," he declared.

That evening, after settling the children with querulous Miss Foggerty, Carrie drove to the restaurant and arrived fifteen minutes early. Frank Colbin was already there, in a stylish business suit, waiting. He took her hand. "You look lovelier than I remembered, Miss Seyers," he said—a remark that might have sounded artificially suave but for the earnestness of his expression.

"Thank you," Carrie replied. She couldn't help noticing that

Mr. Colbin appeared taller and more attractive than her first impression of him. His was a lean, almost gaunt attractiveness, with precise features that appeared sensitive, even poetic.

The hostess led them to a small, linen-covered table accented with a crystal vase of fresh flowers. They were seated and handed large, glossy menus. Frank smiled across at Carrie and remarked, "A fancy place for Madison, wouldn't you agree?"

"Yes, it's beautiful," she replied, gazing admiringly at the ornate chandeliers, then at the velvet wallpaper and handsome paintings.

"Mr. Hawthorne's paintings should be hanging here," Frank noted. "His work is superior to any of these."

"You're right," replied Carrie, "but these are lovely too."

"But you must admit, Mr. Hawthorne's style is unique. You can always spot one of his works."

"I hadn't thought of it, but I suppose you're right."

After they had given their order, Carrie inquired, "How did your job interview go, Mr. Colbin?"

"Call me Frank, please."

"If you'll call me Carrie."

"Is that your given name?"

"Not exactly. My father named me Catherine, and my mother nicknamed me Carrie. Nobody calls me Catherine."

"Oh, but you're much more a Catherine than a Carrie," observed Frank seriously. "Carrie is simple and mundane; Catherine is complex and beautiful."

Carrie laughed self-consciously.

"I'm sorry," said Frank quickly. "I didn't mean to embarrass you. But names are important to me. Would you mind if I call you Catherine?"

"I suppose not," Carrie shrugged. "But back to your job interview—"

Frank tapped his fingers lightly, rhythmically on the tablecloth. His dark eyes took on a bright intensity. "I got the job, Catherine. I begin tomorrow in their training program."

"What will you be doing?"

"Oh, I'm sorry, I assumed you knew. Of course you wouldn't.

I'm working as an agent for the Cosmopolitan Life Insurance Company."

"Have you sold insurance before?"

"No, but I've sold almost everything else." Frank's expression darkened. He picked up a spoon and turned it over and over in his hand, unconsciously. "You probably wonder why a man in his early thirties is starting over now."

"No, it hadn't occurred to me—"

"I did have a good job, an excellent position," Frank continued, his words coming quickly. "I lost someone very important to me, and my life fell apart after that. I couldn't work. I couldn't do anything except think about her."

"I think I understand," murmured Carrie, thinking of Greg.

"You do? You lost someone you loved? Then you know how hard it is to put things back together, to make things right—"

"I've had help in coping," remarked Carrie. "God has given me so much . . . especially strength and comfort when I've needed it."

"Has He?" queried Frank. "That's fine. I'm glad you have such sturdy faith. You seem to be a woman who has her life well under control."

"I hope so. I've tried . . ."

"I'm trying too," said Frank. "I'm dedicating my life to making things right, to bringing about justice . . ."

Carrie smiled, a little puzzled. "With your zeal, Frank, you sound almost like a policeman or a preacher."

"I do have zeal, don't I, Catherine?" His eyes glistened appreciatively. "I feel very strongly about things, about people. I always have. You see that, don't you? I tend to be very single-minded in my purposes."

"What are your purposes, Frank—your goals?" she asked.

Before Frank could reply, a waitress brought them platters of sizzling steaks and baked potatoes with plump mushrooms on the side.

"Oh, I haven't eaten like this in months," marveled Carrie as she cut easily into the red-rare meat.

Frank smiled. "I hope this is just the first of many pleasant evenings with you, Catherine."

During the few remaining weeks of summer, Carrie saw Frank regularly. Although his work took him out of town on weekends, he usually returned in time to sit with her in church on Sunday evenings. She appreciated his company since the children remained home at night with Miss Foggerty. Several times she and Frank had dinner at the Fair Winds restaurant. Occasionally they took a long drive to a neighboring town for an open-air concert, a play, or a county fair.

Carrie enjoyed Frank's company. He was always kind, considerate, and diverting. She had never met anyone quite like him—a serious, intense man who seemed always to be running on nervous energy. He treated her like a queen—as if he had never heard of women's lib. He remained friendly, polite, and solicitous, but, to Carrie's relief, he never made demands for physical contact or intimacy. In fact, he never approached her for more than a casual good-night kiss.

Frank did have one peculiar obsession, however—an insistence that Carrie keep their friendship a secret from her employer and his children. "I don't want them to think I'm trying to spirit you away from them," he explained. "Why create unnecessary anxieties?" So he never came to the Hawthorne house to pick her up, nor did he express any desire to meet her young charges, although he inquired about their health each time she saw him.

Frank maintained his intense interest in Mr. Hawthorne's whereabouts. "You'll call me the minute he returns home, won't you?" he questioned Carrie regularly. "I must see him as soon as he returns . . . so that I can commission him to do that painting for me." When Carrie stared curiously, even at times suspiciously, at him, he would add earnestly, "That painting is very important to me, Catherine. You have no idea of its importance."

On the eighth day of September, Nathan Hawthorne returned home without fanfare or warning. Carrie, wearing an old shirt and jeans, her hair pulled back under a faded bandanna, stood speechless as Nathan entered the house, dropped his suitcase and boomed cheerfully, "Hello, everyone, I'm home!"

Seeing him again, Carrie felt something lurch within her—a positive response, a momentary thrill of pleasure. The reaction surprised and distressed her. Not since Greg had she felt such an emotional response to a man.

Then, when Nathan came and gave her a spontaneous embrace, Carrie's knees nearly buckled. She had forgotten what Nathan's physical presence did to her—or had the feelings magnified during his absence? But how could that be, she wondered, when Frank Colbin had occupied almost all of her attention lately?

"I'm sorry to take you by surprise like this," said Nathan, releasing her and apparently noticing her confusion. "I know I should have telephoned first."

She self-consciously touched her hair. "I must look terrible," she said apologetically.

"You look wonderful," said Nathan. "I can't tell you how I've wanted to be home. I've thought of nothing else for weeks."

"The children will be so glad to see you," she told him as she shook her hair free. "Right now they're in the backyard nursing a sparrow with a broken wing."

"Well, they'll be happy to hear that I'm staying home for a while now. I have enough cash in my pocket to support us for several months. In fact, Woody's quite pleased with the response he's been getting to my work. You should have seen his face when I brought in a dozen new paintings at once. I told him those would have to hold him for a while, because I was going to spend some time with my kids . . . and with you too, Carrie, I hope," he added meaningfully.

"Yes, I'd like that too," she said shyly.

"Starting tonight," he announced. "What should we do—have a barbecue, a picnic, a hike in the woods? What do you want to do?"

Carrie grew flustered. "I—I'm sorry, Nathan, I can't."

"Can't what?"

"I can't plan anything with you and the children tonight."

"Why not?"

"I—I have a sort of—date—for dinner."

"A date?" He stared at her as if he had never quite seen her before. "I don't know why I'm surprised," he sighed after a minute. "A beautiful young girl like you—of course, you'd have dates."

"Miss Foggerty was coming to stay with the children," she said, trying to cover the sudden breech between them.

"*The* Miss Foggerty?"

"Yes, the Wicked Witch of the West, according to Dusty. But, of course, she won't need to come now, with you here." She smiled conciliatorily at him. "I'd like to take a raincheck on that barbecue or picnic if you'll let me. It sounds wonderful."

Nathan gazed back, his eyes narrowing intently. "Your young man—tell me, is it serious?"

"No," said Carrie, too quickly. "We're just friends." She wasn't sure, but she thought she saw an expression of relief cross Nathan's face.

"I'm glad," he said, smiling broadly. "I'd hate to lose you now when I've just found you." As if realizing he was saying more than he intended, he added with a note of humor, "After all, a good housekeeper is hard to find."

Chapter Ten

"I'll be home early," Carrie assured Nathan as she prepared to leave for her date with Frank Colbin. "I really wish I didn't have to go," she told the children sincerely as they ran to her for good-bye kisses.

"Then stay home," said Dusty with his usual practicality. "Tell the Invisible Man you can't go."

"It wouldn't be nice to break a date," explained Carrie.

"Invisible Man?" echoed Nathan. "What kind of name is that?"

"That's what the kids call him," laughed Carrie sheepishly.

"He's invisible," insisted Dusty. "We never see him."

"What's his name?" inquired Nathan.

"Oh, you wouldn't know him," said Carrie evasively, recalling her promise to Frank.

"Well, I'll wait up for you if you don't mind," said Nathan as he walked her to the door. "I'll have hot chocolate and bran muffins waiting."

"You don't have to do that—"

"I want to. I'm eager to talk to you again about your poet David. I've become rather well acquainted with him these past few weeks."

"I'm glad," said Carrie. "I'll look forward to our talk together."

"Good." He smiled at her. "I can't think of a better combination right now than hot chocolate and warm conversation."

A short time later, as Carrie drove toward the Fair Winds restaurant, her heart and thoughts remained at home with Nathan. More than once she considered turning around and going back, but she couldn't hurt Frank. He had been so kind to her these past few weeks. But she hadn't realized until now how different her feelings were for these two men in her life. She felt comfortable with Frank, as she did with her father or brother. But Nathan—how could she express the effect he had on her, the way he made her feel when he came near? Was it possible that she was falling in love with Nathan Hawthorne?

Moments after Carrie and Frank were seated in the restaurant, he looked closely at her and said, "Something's on your mind, Catherine."

"Yes," she admitted. "Nathan Hawthorne came home today."

Frank sat forward with a sudden, startled gesture. His pale complexion blanched to a sickly white. "Nathan? He's home?"

"Yes. He arrived just a couple of hours ago," she responded. "What's wrong, Frank? You look . . . ill."

Frank sat back in his chair and stared into space. His fingers tapped the table with a vigorous, staccato rhythm. "Nathan," he murmured under his breath. "At last . . . at last."

Frank's brows pinched his eyes in his usual anxious expression. But there was more in his face tonight—a bizarre quality that disturbed Carrie. His smooth, narrow cheekbones tightened subtly, and there was a new animation to his features—a strange blend of barely suppressed anger, excitement, and anticipation.

"Something's wrong, Frank," Carrie pressed. A waitress brought their soup and salad then so she lowered her voice. "Please, tell me what it is. What has you so upset?"

"Nothing," he replied curtly. "For the first time in a long time everything is right."

"But you won't tell me what it is?"

"Yes, I will, I want to. I must tell you—tonight. But not here. Somewhere private."

"We could go for a little drive after dinner. I can leave my car in the parking lot like we sometimes do."

"All right," agreed Frank. He poked nervously at his salad. "But I'm not hungry now. Are you hungry?"

"Not very. Maybe we should just finish our soup and salad, and go."

"A good idea, Catherine. Yes, That would be fine."

A half hour later, Frank pulled his automobile over onto a grassy sward beside a lake several miles outside of Madison. Dance music wafted from a pavilion across the water. The breeze coming in the open car windows was cool, refreshing. Carrie thought fleetingly that this would be the ideal romantic spot—if she were with Nathan.

Thinking of Nathan, she recalled that he was at home waiting for her. They would have a lovely, leisurely conversation tonight over hot chocolate and warm bran muffins. But first, Frank had to have his say. She was hoping he would be brief.

"What did you want to tell me, Frank?" she questioned, being careful not to sound impatient.

Frank had his arms crossed on the steering wheel; his fingers thumped nervously. "Oh, Catherine, Catherine," he said with almost a moan. "Where do I begin? Where?" He looked imploringly at her. "You must understand, Catherine, why I haven't been exactly honest with you. You must believe it has nothing to do with you."

Carrie felt repulsed by Frank's sudden emotional outburst, but she tried to sound sympathetic as she murmured, "I don't understand, Frank. Honest about what?"

"About my reasons for being in Madison, my reason for wanting to see your Mr. Nathan Hawthorne."

Carrie shook her head, perplexed. "What does Nathan Hawthorne have to do with this?"

"Everything," said Frank, his voice high-pitched and breathy. "He has everything to do with this."

"You're confusing me, Frank. I don't know what you're talking about."

He paused and looked at her. His expression sobered. "Do you remember when I told you I had lost someone I loved?"

"Yes, of course."

"Well, that someone was my sister Pamela." His voice softened. "She was the loveliest woman I've ever known. Blond hair, exquisite features. A princess, a jewel, too good for this earth. She should have had the perfect life, the best of everything."

Frank cleared his throat to ease the emotion in his voice, then continued. "When Pamela was nineteen, she married a man, a worthless, unpredictable fellow. She was so sure he would make her happy. They had two children, a nice enough home, I suppose, but she wasn't satisfied with him. She realized she loved someone else, someone who was worthy of her. But when her husband found out, he . . . he murdered her!"

Carrie emitted a sudden, incredulous gasp. "Oh, no, Frank. How terrible!"

Frank buried his head in his hands and sobbed. Carrie instinctively held out her hand to him in an awkward attempt to offer some measure of comfort.

After a moment, he gained control of himself and fumbled in his pocket for a handkerchief. "I'm so sorry, Catherine," he said huskily. "I've never given in to the pain before. Please forgive me."

Carrie sat back but kept her hand on Frank's arm. "Don't apologize, Frank. You shouldn't be ashamed of showing your grief."

"I loved her more than life itself, Catherine. We were always very close."

"There's just one thing I don't understand, Frank," persisted Carrie. "What does your sister's death have to do with my employer?"

Frank's dark eyes hardened chillingly. He spoke slowly and with stabbing precision. "My sister's husband, the man who murdered her, was Nathan Havers—the man you know as Nathan Hawthorne."

Carrie stared at him uncomprehendingly. As the meaning of Frank's words took hold, she shook her head in bewilderment and uttered, "Nathan?"

"Yes," insisted Frank. "I've spent months tracking him down, tracing him here to Madison. Without a doubt, your Mr. Hawthorne is Pamela's killer."

Carrie slowly removed her hand from Frank's arm. "Let me get this straight," she said. "You mean you—you used *me* to locate Nathan?"

"I had to find him, Catherine. You must understand. The man is a fugitive from justice, a killer."

"Don't say that," pleaded Carrie, drawing back instinctively. "You don't know what you're saying. You've made a terrible mistake."

"No, Catherine. It's all true. I can prove it." He reached into the glove compartment and produced a packet of yellowed news clippings from *The Springfield Gazette*. She flipped through them gingerly, and, by the dim overhead light, read the headlines: *Local Woman Found Murdered, Area Man Held in Wife's Death, Havers to Stand Trial, Accused Killer Jumps Bail, Havers Escapes with Offspring, Murdered Woman's Children Still Missing*.

One clipping showed a blurred photo of a man who could have been Nathan but just as likely was not. "There's nothing here to prove that my employer is this man," she said fiercely.

"He *is* Nathan Havers, and his children are Dustin and Melinda Havers, your young charges," Frank told her with equal firmness.

Carrie was about to argue further, when something from her memory assailed her with a haunting, pulse-stopping realization. It was Mindy's determined, little-girl voice saying, "My name is Mindy . . . *Havers*."

Chapter Eleven

Carrie stared defiantly at Frank. "Even if my employer is your Nathan Havers, you haven't proved he murdered his wife," she challenged. "The man I know is too kind and gentle to harm anyone."

Frank's eyes glinted like steel in the pale light as he replied, "The police found him with her just after it happened. There was no one else around, no sign of forced entry. The evidence against Nathan Havers is overwhelming."

Carrie found herself fighting back angry tears. She couldn't believe this was happening. How did a pleasant evening with such promise suddenly turn into a nightmare? "I still don't believe he did it," she said hotly.

"Then why did he run away, jump bail? Why did he steal his own children from their grandparents'—my parents'—home? If he has nothing to conceal, why has he hidden these past nine months?"

"He hasn't hidden. He's been away painting."

"He changed his name," countered Frank. "He deposited his children in a house in the middle of nowhere. No one ever sees him; no one knows who he is."

For the moment Carrie couldn't think of any more arguments. "Then how—did *you* find him?" she demanded.

Frank's expression assumed an animation, almost a brilliance, which Carrie could compare only to an evangelistic zeal. He said fervently, "I made it my supreme goal to bring Nathan Havers to justice, to see to it that he pays for his crime. When the police could find no trace of him, I began scouting art galleries across the country. I knew his only means of income would be his paintings, and I knew when I found his paintings, I would find him. Finally I came upon Sherwood Garrett's gallery near here and only a day's drive from Springfield. You know the rest.''

"What are you going to do now?'' Carrie asked, her tone subdued.

"In the morning I will notify the police that I have found Havers. From there on it will be their job.''

"You mean they'll come and arrest him?''

"Yes . . . and that's where you come in, Catherine.''

"Me?'' she cried. ''I don't want any part of this!''

"You must do me a favor,'' persisted Frank. ''I don't want my niece and nephew to see their father arrested. They've suffered enough already. I want you to take them away for the day, on a picnic or something.''

"But what about when we get home . . . and their father isn't there?''

"I'll be there, and I'll take them back to their grandparents' home where they belong.''

Carrie shook her head despairingly. ''They belong with their father.'' She bit her lip to keep back a sob.

Frank took her hand and held it consolingly. ''I'm sorry, Catherine. I wish I could have spared you all of this.''

"Then why didn't you, Frank?'' Carrie looked up at him with growing comprehension and carefully withdrew her hand. ''Our friendship, Frank, all the evenings we've spent together these past few weeks—it was all a sham, wasn't it? You were seeing me just so you could keep tabs on Nathan.''

"No, Catherine. At first, perhaps that was my only intention. But over the weeks I've grown very fond of you.'' He reached again for her hand. ''I hope you care for me too—and I hope we can still be friends.''

"I don't know. I don't know anything right now, except that I want to be alone.''

"All right, Catherine.'' Frank slowly shifted his position and reached for the ignition key. "I'll drive you back to town for your car."

A half hour later, as Carrie sat in her automobile in the Fair Winds parking lot and watched Frank drive away, she felt as alone as she had the day she watched Woody Garrett drive away from the Hawthorne house without her. For several minutes she sat unmoving, her hands folded on the steering wheel, her eyes staring ahead, unseeing. She was trying desperately to put the pieces together, to fit Frank's incredible accusation into the scheme of reality. She pictured Nathan—the man she was on the verge of loving. He couldn't possibly be guilty of such a hideous deed. But why was he leading such a secretive existence? Why were there so many things about him that didn't add up? At the moment, Carrie deeply resented both men—Frank for using her to reach Nathan, and Nathan for being so mysterious that she could doubt him.

Finally, Carrie gave in to the tears gathering just below the surface of her barely controlled emotions. "Oh, God, what am I going to do?" she sobbed. "Help me! Help Nathan and the children."

She considered driving home to Claremont, back to the loving security her parents would gladly provide. But what would she tell them? Still, how could she face Nathan and the children? What would she say? What would Nathan do?

Even as she wrestled with such agonizing questions, she found herself starting the automobile, pulling out of the parking lot, and taking the familiar road back to the Hawthorne house. Or was it the *Havers* house?"

It was nearly eleven-thirty when Carrie quietly unlocked the front door and went inside. The house was silent. One living room light was burning. She hoped against hope that Nathan had gone up to bed so that she wouldn't have to face him until morning.

But before she could even set down her purse, Nathan came striding out from the kitchen toward her. He took hold of her shoulders with an energy that left her speechless. "Where have you been?" he demanded, searching her face anxiously.

"I told you I had a date," she replied weakly.

His strong hands eased their grip and his expression softened.

"I was worried sick," he told her. "You said you'd make it an early evening. I was looking for you around nine. I thought there must have been an accident."

"No, I—we were delayed. I didn't realize it was so late."

"Well, no harm done," he said relentingly, "except that the hot chocolate boiled over and the bran muffins may have dried out a bit. But you're safe. That's the important thing."

He stopped and looked at her more closely. "You've been crying."

"No, Nathan, I'm fine, really."

"You don't look fine. You look like somebody just knocked the world out from under you." He paused, his brows knitting suspiciously. "Did that fellow try something? If he did, I'll—"

"No, Nathan, it's nothing like that." Carrie turned away. "Please, Nathan, I'm very tired. I just want to go upstairs to bed."

He sounded hurt as he questioned, "But what about our talk?"

"It'll have to be another time. Good night." She started to walk toward the stairs, but his voice stopped her.

"Carrie," he said forcefully, "something's wrong. What is it?"

She refused to look him in the eye, until he walked over, faced her squarely and turned her chin up to him. "Tell me what happened, Carrie," he insisted.

She began to cry.

He threw up his hands in a gesture of frustration. "Did I do this—or is it this other guy who's making you cry? How can I help if I don't know what's going on?"

Carrie dried her eyes and made an effort to compose herself. "I'm sorry," she told Nathan. "I shouldn't have cried. It's not something I can talk about."

Nathan guided her into the living room and gently sat her down. He took a seat across from her. "I'm here, Carrie. I'm willing to listen."

Carrie's thoughts raced. Did she dare confront Nathan with the truth? She had always been taught the importance of honesty. The Bible said, *The truth shall make you free*. She reasoned, if Nathan actually were the man in Frank's newspaper clipping, wasn't it possible that things would go better for him if he gave himself up? Perhaps he could even go back voluntarily and clear his name.

"Carrie? Did you hear me?" Nathan repeated. "I'm listening."

"Yes, Nathan," she replied cautiously. "I do want to talk. I— I want to tell you whom I was out with tonight."

"All right, go ahead. Who was it?"

She took a deep breath and said, "A man who says he's your brother-in-law."

"My brother-in-law?" Nathan repeated incredulously. "What's his name?"

In a halting whisper, she answered, "Frank . . . Frank Colbin."

Chapter Twelve

Nathan stared at her as if he had been struck by gunshot. Carrie felt herself flinching under his fierce scrutiny. His voice raw with emotion, he demanded, "What sort of game are you playing, Carrie?"

"It's no game, Nathan," she said miserably. "It's just that I— I have to know the truth."

"What truth?"

"About you . . . and your wife."

Nathan's tone took on a sullen edge. "It sounds like we both have some explaining to do." He looked at her, raising one eyebrow critically. "Tell me one thing, Miss Seyers. Did Frank send you here to spy on me?"

"No, of course not! I never even knew him until he came to the house looking for you a couple of months ago."

"Why did you wait so long to tell me you were seeing him?"

"Because I didn't know until tonight who he was . . . or who you were."

"Is that the truth?"

"Yes."

"All right," he said seriously, "then you tell me the whole story about Frank." He paused meaningfully. "And I'll tell you my story."

Carrie explained briefly how she had met Frank Colbin and of his supposed interest in commissioning a painting by Nathan. She concluded with Frank's shocking revelation and his plans to notify the police of Nathan's whereabouts.

"Are you saying the police could show up here tonight!" he exclaimed, his face flushing with anger.

"No," she said quickly. "He's going to wait until tomorrow when the children and I are away from the house." She realized too late that she was speaking out of turn, foolishly revealing too much.

Nathan stood up and paced the room, scowling. "How convenient that Frank has your cooperation in this little conspiracy against me," he retorted.

"He doesn't!" cried Carrie. "I told him I want nothing to do with this."

"Do you believe him—that I'm a—a murderer?"

"Oh, Nathan, you've always been so kind, so good with the children!"

He came over and stared down severely at her. "Do you believe I murdered my wife, Carrie? Answer me!"

She looked up beseechingly at him. "Oh, Nathan, I don't know what to believe. Please tell me what happened."

He turned away sharply, his lips curling in contempt. "Why should I? You've already made up your mind. Besides, there isn't time now."

She stood and approached him cautiously. "What do you mean?"

He pivoted and glared at her. "The children and I must leave. Tonight."

"But you can't just go. You can't keep running."

"Can't I?"

"The children can't live like that. It's not fair to them."

"Very little in this world is fair, Carrie."

"But if you'd give yourself up, if you'd voluntarily go back and face the charges, perhaps you could clear your name."

"Or perhaps I'd end up spending the rest of my life in prison," he countered. "I could even face the death penalty."

"Oh, Nathan, no!"

He gripped her shoulders and searched her eyes with a raw

urgency. "I swear before God, Carrie, I never harmed my wife. I adored her. She was everything to me. There's not a day that passes that I don't die a little inside without her. But there's no way I can convince you of my innocence tonight. You'll have to decide for yourself." He strode to the kitchen, with Carrie close behind.

"What am I supposed to do?" she asked in a small voice.

"Whatever you please. Stay here. Go home. Come with us." He began loading boxes and cans of food into a cardboard carton.

"Go with you? Oh, I couldn't!"

"Then take the car you've been using and go home."

"But who will care for the children?"

"I will. I'll manage somehow." He looked at her and added, "If you want to help, you can go pack their bags while I get the dishes, sheets and towels."

"Isn't there anything I can say to persuade you to stay—?"

"No, Carrie. You've said too much already."

Reluctantly Carrie turned and went upstairs to gather the youngsters' belongings. Tears slid silently down her cheeks as she gazed at the sleeping children, their faces so innocent and trusting. She longed to take them in her arms and protect them from all the ugliness and pain the world had to offer. But now it looked as if she would never see them again. She wouldn't even have any way of keeping in touch, or of knowing they were safe and well.

"Oh, dear Jesus," she whispered aloud, "I can't let them go like this. I just can't."

She realized then what she had to do. It was a brash, unthinkable idea. She would be putting herself in danger, making herself vulnerable to countless unknown possibilities, perhaps even breaking the law. Carrie's conscience screamed against the plan, but the devotion she felt to Nathan and the children at this moment overcame reason. If Nathan is guilty of his wife's death, the children need me more than ever, she argued. If he is innocent of the charge, he deserves my loyalty and assistance.

She made her decision. She would go with Nathan and the children, wherever they went, regardless of what they faced.

Quickly, resolutely, Carrie packed the children's clothing and toys, then went to her own room and gathered her things. As she carried the suitcases into the hall, Nathan came from his room with his luggage. "Our things are ready," she told him.

He looked at her suitcases and said, "So you're taking the car and going home?"

"No, Nathan. I'm coming with you."

He looked momentarily quizzical; then a faint smile played on his lips. "Does this mean you believe me? You trust me?"

"It means I can't just walk away from the children. They need me. But I still think you're wrong to keep running."

His smile vanished. "What if I say you can't come with us?"

"Then I'll go home," she said quietly, "But my prayers will go with you."

"If you come with us, Carrie, I can't promise it'll be easy. I can't guarantee your safety."

"I'll take my chances," she replied, more bravely than she felt.

He took her luggage and started down the stairs, calling back, "Are the children awake yet?"

"No. I wanted them to sleep as long as possible."

"Well, get them up and dressed. It's after one. I want to be on the road in fifteen minutes."

Carrie entered the children's room and knelt by their beds. "Oh, God, please take care of us," she prayed. She felt herself trembling as she added, "Keep the children safe . . . and make Nathan see he has to stop running."

Dusty stirred at the sound of her voice and groggily opened one eye. "Is it time to get up, Carrie?" he mumbled.

"Yes, Dusty," she answered quietly. "We have to go away."

"Away?"

"Yes, on a little trip."

Dusty sat up in bed and rubbed his eyes with his fists. "But it's still dark outside, Carrie."

"I know, Dusty. But your daddy wants to start our trip early, while the traffic is light and the air is cool."

"But I'm tired."

"I know, honey. But you can go back to sleep in the van."

Dusty clambered out of bed, went over and shook his sister.

"Come on, Mindy, wake up. We're going away again. Daddy's playing hide-and-go-seek like we did at Grandma's."

"I don't want to play," Mindy complained sleepily, burrowing her head under the covers."

Dusty gazed woefully at Carrie. "Do we have to play? Daddy's game isn't any fun."

"Why isn't it?" she ventured.

Dusty's lower lip quivered. "Because nobody ever finds us."

Chapter Thirteen

Throughout the night Nathan drove in dogged silence, heading west. The children slept fitfully in the crowded back of the weathered van while Carrie sat unmoving in the front seat, her head resting uncomfortably against the door. She felt numb, yet she couldn't stop shivering. Over and over she prayed, "Lord, don't let me be making a mistake," but the repetition did little to relieve her mental burden.

She wondered now about all sorts of random things. What would Woody Garrett think when he found the Hawthorne house deserted? (He would certainly check on her when she didn't answer his weekly call.) Would Nathan permit Carrie to contact her parents? What would they think if she suddenly just "disappeared"? What would life be like now that she and Nathan and the children were living like fugitives? She had placed herself in a no-win situation, but last night there had seemed no other choice. Now, with dawn breaking on an unfamiliar horizon, she wasn't so sure.

At the first glint of sunlight, Dusty awoke and whined, "Daddy, I have to go to the bathroom."

"Me too," Mindy echoed sleepily.

After a moment's reluctance, Nathan pulled off the highway and found the nearest service station. In the restroom, Carrie splashed cold water on her face and brushed her teeth to get rid of the foul taste in her mouth. Her muscles ached from sitting so long in a cramped position; her eyes felt grainy from lack of sleep. She wished desperately that she were at home in bed in Claremont, or even in the lumpy old bed back at Nathan's rented house. Staring in the dingy mirror at her wan, rumpled reflection, she reminded herself that she wasn't cut out for this sort of thing. Her sister Kara was the daring, adventuresome one. Carrie had always preferred a sane, sensible existence. Ironically, it looked as if her life from now on would be anything but predictable.

Once they were on the road again, the two children began to bicker and complain.

"I'm hungry," whined Mindy.

"She's taking up all the room," grumbled Dusty.

"My tummy hurts!"

"I can't see out the window."

"I'm starving to death!"

Dusty leaned forward on the front seat. "I'm tired of riding. When are we going to get there?"

"Get where?" questioned Carrie.

"Wherever we're going."

Carrie looked at Nathan. "I'm wondering that too. Where are we going?"

"I don't know," he replied crossly. "The West Coast, maybe."

"The West Coast? That'll take a couple more days of driving!"

"I know."

"The children are tired already. And so am I."

He glanced at her. "You asked to come, remember?" More gently he added, "We'll stop somewhere tonight."

"You mean you plan to drive all day?" cried Carrie. "How can you? You haven't had any sleep!"

"I'll manage." He offered a mild smile. "If I get too tired, I'll let you drive."

"What about eating? The children are hungry."

"We'll pick something up at a drive-through restaurant. Keep your eyes open for one."

"You mean a fast-food place?"

"Yes. We'll grab something and eat while we travel."

"Oh, Nathan, no. The children need good, nourishing food."

"There isn't time," he said sharply.

Minutes later he pulled into a Quick Burger restaurant and ordered four breakfasts to go. Everyone ate in grudging silence as Nathan pulled back with a screech and a squeal onto the highway.

"I want to go home," Mindy whined when they had traveled another hour.

"Me too," grunted Dusty. "The van's too warm and the road's bumpy. I'm going to throw up."

Nathan glared back irritably in the rearview mirror and snapped, "You will *not* throw up, young man!"

"I think Dusty means it," said Carrie worriedly.

Nathan swerved over to the shoulder of the highway, climbed out of the van, and led Dusty over to a grassy knoll. The two were back shortly, Nathan frowning, Dusty pale and sweaty.

"Feel better?" Carrie asked the boy.

He nodded as he climbed in and curled up in the back of the van.

At two, against Carrie's protests, Nathan stopped at another drive-through restaurant for lunch; then, out of sheer necessity, he turned the wheel over to Carrie. "I'm dead on my feet," he told her. "You drive, and stay on the highway heading west."

Carrie obeyed automatically, wondering for a moment if she might find an opportunity to telephone her parents. She couldn't bear the idea of them being frantic with worry, thinking she had been kidnapped—or worse.

But as the hours passed and the highway stretched ahead in a gray, monotonous ribbon, Carrie discarded the thought of calling home. What if Nathan awoke and caught her on the phone? He might suspect that she was turning him in, and drive off, leaving her stranded in this desert wasteland.

She hadn't noticed when they had left the lush, variegated scenery of the Midwest behind for the endless, airless brown desert. She wondered where they would spend the night. Civilization appeared only in rare, sporadic clumps—a gas station here, a faded, wind-beaten cafe there, a random clutch of dwellings with perhaps an inauspicious—and unappealing—motel.

It was just such a forbidding place that Nathan pulled into late that evening. He would have been content to drive all night, since he had slept well through the afternoon while Carrie drove. But Carrie and the children emitted such a wail of gloom at the prospect of a second night coiled like snails in the crowded van that Nathan grudgingly agreed to find them a motel.

Nathan's motel selection prompted almost as much dismay as had the prospect of sleeping again in the vehicle. But Carrie quelled her misgivings and waited silently while Nathan entered the cubicle of an office to secure the necessary rooms.

He returned a minute later with a key and said, "We're down this way. Room 3A."

Carrie looked at him in bewilderment. "One room?" she nearly bleated. "I assumed you would get two."

He gazed at her with weary perturbation and said, "I couldn't, Carrie. Only one was available. Do you want it or not?"

"Yes, yes, of course I do," she replied fervently. "But what did you tell the man?"

"Nothing. I registered us as Mr. and Mrs. Hampton . . . with our two children."

"That's dishonest," she said in a small, abashed voice.

"Oh, I don't think so. We're the perfect family, wouldn't you say?" She couldn't miss the bitter irony in his voice.

The room wasn't quite as dreary as Carrie had feared. It contained marine-blue carpeting and drapes, two double beds, a broken TV set, and a reasonably tidy bathroom.

While the youngsters raced each other for the bathroom, Carrie glanced around the room, then looked questioningly at Nathan.

Reading her unspoken query, he directed, "You and Mindy take that bed, Dusty and I'll take this one."

"There's not much privacy," she observed timidly.

"No, there's not," he agreed, and began to unbutton his shirt.

Before Carrie could protest, the children scampered out of the bathroom in their pajamas. "Do we got to brush our teeth?" Dusty quizzed. "I'm too tired."

"You can skip it this once," said Nathan, pulling back the bed covers for the boy. "You here, son, and Mindy over there," he told them.

"Oh, boy, I get to sleep with Carrie!" exulted the girl.

Carrie was touched. Hardly anything elicited such verbal enthusiasm from the child. She went over, kissed the youngsters good night, and prayed quietly with them while Nathan was in the bathroom.

Both children were sleeping soundly by the time Nathan finished his shower and emerged, robed, rubbing his hair with a towel. "Boy, I needed that," he remarked, sounding more relaxed than he had since yesterday. He looked with curiosity at Carrie. "Have you just been sitting there reading that Gideon Bible? Aren't you going to get ready for bed?"

She returned the Bible to its place on the bedside table, then glanced self-consciously at Nathan. "I'm not accustomed to running around in my nightgown in front of strangers," she announced, hating the prissy tone that had crept into her voice.

"You're not going to run around, Carrie. You're going to bed."

"Well, you know what I mean," she argued. "This isn't exactly a proper situation for either one of us."

He smiled grimly and murmured, "Regardless of what you think of me after talking with my brother-in-law, I assure you your virtue is safe with me."

Carrie reluctantly took some things from her suitcase and started for the bathroom. She looked back at Nathan and said, "I'll probably be a while. You don't have to wait up."

The bath felt wonderful after the tense, uncomfortable hours in the van. Carrie relaxed, letting the water soothe her tired body. As she tried to decipher the problems facing the family, her thoughts slowed, and her mind told her she was too tired to think clearly.

Carrie finally stepped out of the tub, gave her skin a brisk rubdown, and dressed in comfortable clothes for the next day's traveling. She glanced at Nathan as she walked to her bed. He looked as if he'd been sleeping for hours.

Chapter Fourteen

When Carrie awoke the next morning, she couldn't recall where she was. Then she saw Mindy sleeping peacefully beside her, and memories of the past thirty-six hours swept back with alarming clarity. She rolled over and glanced at the next bed. For an instant, panic struck. Only Dusty was there. Where was Nathan? Had he left without them?

No. Even as she listened intently, she heard water running in the bathroom. Finally, the door opened and Nathan emerged, freshly shaven, dressed in an attractive sport shirt and slacks.

Nathan slipped his wallet and keys into his pocket and walked to the door. "I'm going out to get gas and pick up a few groceries," he said. "That'll give you and the kids a chance to get ready."

Carrie sat up and stared at him. "You—you will come back?"

He gave her a curious glance. "Of course. Did you think I wouldn't?"

She laughed self-consciously. "I'm sorry. It was a dumb thing to say. We'll be ready when you get back."

He opened the door. "Just to let you know, Carrie, we won't be making any more motel stops."

"We won't?"

"We'll take turns driving. If we drive straight through, we should be able to reach Los Angeles by tomorrow afternoon."

"Why Los Angeles?"

"It's a big city, one we can get lost in for a while."

72

"What will we do there?"

He shrugged. "We'll figure that out tomorrow."

Nathan was true to his word. Except for bathroom, fast-food, and fuel stops, the van sped on toward the California border. That night Carrie and Nathan spelled each other, one behind the wheel while the other caught catnaps in the back of the van.

Once, toward morning, as Carrie took Nathan's place behind the wheel, she broached the subject uppermost on her mind. They had stopped on a lonely span of desert highway. The earth seemed as silent and empty as the sky. In the predawn shadows, Nathan's face looked haggard, drawn. She felt his sense of futility, the utter exhaustion of running for his life against impossible odds.

She touched his arm and said, "Nathan, it won't work. We can't keep running like this. Why don't you contact the authorities, tell them your side of the story? A lawyer could help you, Nathan. If you could just clear your name, you and Dusty and Mindy would be able to live a normal life. You owe them that, Nathan."

He glared at her. "You don't know anything about it, Carrie. Giving myself up would be like signing my own death sentence. Is that what you want—two innocent children left fatherless as well as motherless?"

"Of course it's not what I want!" she cried. "I just don't know how long we'll be able to survive under this kind of pressure—"

"I've survived nearly a year already," he replied bitterly. More gently, he said, "Get some sleep, Carrie. You'll need it tomorrow."

At three the next afternoon, they crossed the San Bernardino Mountains and caught their first glimpse of the Los Angeles basin.

"It's so big, so sprawling," Carrie murmured. "The city looks like it goes on forever."

"That's where we're going to lose ourselves, Carrie. We're going to become part of all the 'faceless humanity' down there."

Carrie didn't reply. She felt a dark, gnawing sensation that she shouldn't even be a part of this dismal escapade, this bizarre flight from all she knew to be sane and sensible. She uttered a silent prayer and wondered if God would listen to her now. Yes, He would; His love wasn't based on her own goodness. Still, her daily fellowship with the Lord depended on her obedience to His Word. She wondered whom she was obeying? God? Nathan? Or some mysterious instinct of her own heart?

"What now?" she asked Nathan as he took a freeway off-ramp onto a busy eight-lane city street.

"We look for a place to park our goods—an apartment somewhere."

"How do you know where to go?"

"I don't. When I see something I like, we'll stop."

An hour later he pulled up beside a Spanish-style apartment complex surrounded by palm trees and tropical greenery. He spread a worn map across the steering wheel and studied it.

"Where are we?" ventured Carrie.

"Telegraph Road."

"What city?"

"I'm not sure. They all run together. According to the map, I'd guess we're in the industrial section of a city called Downey."

"That apartment looks nice from here, but I'd be afraid to have the children play near this busy street."

Nathan folded the map. "Well, let's check the place out, okay?"

"The children are napping," noted Carrie. "I'll stay here with them."

"No," said Nathan. "Wake them. We'll all go in. After all, we've all got to live here, so everyone should have a vote on it."

Before she could rouse the youngsters, he warned, "Keep in mind, Carrie, we're not the Havers, nor even the Hawthornes—"

"Then who are we?" Carrie cried in exasperation.

"The Hamptons."

"I won't lie," Carrie shot back.

"I'm not asking you to. I'll do the talking."

Sullenly Carrie thought that her entire existence was becoming a lie, whether she uttered a word or not.

The manager of the Polynesian Winds apartments was a squat, bosomy woman in a Hawaiian print shirt and polyester slacks. "Can I help you? I'm Mrs. Fernandez," she said, bustling about, waving thick hands with long, fake, red nails. Before Nathan could utter more than, "We're from out of town and looking for—"

Mrs. Fernandez announced, "I have just the apartment for you—a lovely little two-bedroom with kitchenette. It's not large, I admit, but it's certainly comfortable."

She beamed at Dusty and Mindy and talked on, "Some places don't cater to children, you know, even though the law says no discrimination, but people have ways of getting around that, of making folks with kids feel unwelcome. But not me. I figure children have their place and they've got to live somewhere. Would you like to see it?"

Carrie looked up, puzzled. "See what?"

"The apartment, of course."

"Yes, we would, Mrs. Fernandez," replied Nathan, masking an amused smile by rubbing his lip.

The apartment was just as Mrs. Fernandez had described—small but comfortable, with spindly Early American furniture and plastic-framed prints on the walls.

"We won't need those," said Nathan, barely hiding his contempt. "I have my own paintings."

"He's an artist," Carrie explained.

"Oh, how wonderful!" bubbled Mrs. Fernandez. "I just love real paintings! They're so—so rare. I simply must see your work, Mr.—"

"Hampton," said Nathan.

Carrie looked away.

Before the afternoon was over, Nathan had arranged to exchange one of his paintings for the first and last month's rent, plus the cleaning deposit. As he and Carrie unloaded the van, he exulted, "At this rate our money will last longer than I expected."

"But paintings won't pay for groceries and electricity and a hundred other things we'll need."

Nathan propped a box of canned goods on his knee, then lifted the carton out of the van. "We'll get by, Carrie. Trust me."

"I'm trying to," she murmured. She gave Nathan a perturbed glance. "Mrs. Fernandez thinks we're married, you know."

Nathan returned a cavalier wink. "There are worse things than being married to me."

"I'll never know!" she snapped, pivoting away from the van

with an armload of toys and household supplies. A bag of Dusty's marbles fell to the ground and burst open. Marbles ran in every direction. Carrie looked back helplessly at Nathan. He squelched a smirk.

Carrie threatened, "If you make some dumb joke about me losing my marbles, I'll clobber you!"

Nathan began to laugh. In spite of herself, Carrie laughed too. They were forced to set down their burdens and compose themselves before continuing on to their apartment.

Dusty and Mindy were in the courtyard, exploring. "There's a swimming pool!" Dusty cried gleefully. "Can I swim, Dad? Can I please?"

"It's late and it's too cold," said Carrie.

"No, it's not. Come feel, Carrie. The water's warm, and it has lights and everything!"

"Not tonight, sport," said Nathan. "But first thing in the morning I'll race you to the pool, okay?"

"Me too!" chimed Mindy.

"Not me," said Carrie. "I'm sleeping in!"

That night, as Carrie put fresh sheets on the beds and stocked the cupboards with groceries, she had to admit she felt relieved to be off the road and settled down again—even if it was an unfamiliar apartment with cracker-box rooms and cookie-cutter furniture. It would do for now. It would do until she figured out some way to convince Nathan to give himself up.

Her ruminations were interrupted as Nathan entered the kitchen with two pajama-clad youngsters under his arms. "Say good night to Carrie," he instructed them. They sprang eagerly into Carrie's arms and smothered her with kisses.

Mindy took Carrie's hand and gave a tug. "Come tuck me in. Daddy says we get the bedroom closest to the bathroom 'cause we spend so much time there."

"I plead innocent!" Nathan exclaimed, throwing up his hands. "But I did say you and Mindy could have the front bedroom. I figured it would be more convenient."

"In that case, I'll ignore the insult," laughed Carrie.

During the next week, as life took on a pleasant predictability,

Carrie relaxed and enjoyed the California sunshine. Nathan seemed determined to make up to his children for all the months he had been away. One day he and Carrie took the children to the beach where they romped in the brisk ocean waves until sunset; another day they drove to the San Diego zoo where they walked for hours, staring down elephants, waving at sky-high giraffes, and making faces at droopy-eyed orangutangs and swinging, rubber-legged chimpanzees.

At Nathan's insistence they splurged one day and drove to Disneyland, where they wandered with fascination through Fantasy Land, Adventure Land, Bear Country, and New Orleans Square. Even Nathan rode the King Arthur Carousel and the Casey Jr. Circus Train. They devoured hot dogs and French fries at the Tomorrowland Terrace and bought stuffed animals at the Main Street Emporium.

At dusk they had Monte Cristo sandwiches in the quaint, dimly lit Blue Bayou restaurant. While the exhausted children slept in their chairs, Carrie and Nathan slipped into warm conversation, nearly forgetting their food. As if touched by the magic of their surroundings, they talked easily of their childhoods, their hopes and dreams.

"When I was a kid, I desperately wanted Walt Disney to discover me and take me back to his studios to draw for him," Nathan remarked with a chuckle. "I spent hours drawing every day so that I would be ready when he came for me."

"What happened?" asked Carrie.

Nathan drummed his fingers lightly on the tablecloth. "He never came. I grew up."

"Then why didn't you go find him?"

"Disney was gone by then, and so was my love for cartooning. I guess you have to maintain some of the mystique of childhood for that sort of thing."

"And you didn't?"

"No. Raw reality hit early for me. My folks divorced when I was twelve. Dad went his way and died a few years later—of alcoholism, I suspect."

"And your mother?"

"She married again, but my stepfather and I never got along. I left home at eighteen without even saying good-bye. I attended college, then the Chicago Art Institute, and studied for two years in Europe, looking for my artistic niche—you know, trying to develop my own unique style. By the time I came home, Mother was ill. Dying."

"I'm sorry," said Carrie.

Nathan's voice grew husky. "Mom was incredible, the way she handled it. She had become what you'd call a godly woman. She rarely complained. Just said it was all in the Lord's hands. I couldn't see it that way. We had only a few special weeks together before her death."

Carrie touched his hand.

Nathan sipped his mint julep, then said, "Now it's your turn. What sort of extraordinary childhood did you have?"

Carrie pushed back her chestnut hair offhandedly. "My childhood was apple-pie normal. I grew up in the Midwest. My dad is a newspaper editor. I have a terrific mother and an okay brother. I've always liked to write, but I never gave it serious consideration until this year."

"That's it? No skeletons in closets or deep, dark passions?"

"Not a one. Except—"

"I knew it!"

"It's not me. It's—well, when I was seventeen I discovered I had a half-sister, Kara Strickland. Not even my dad knew about her."

"Now that sounds like a story. I bet there was the devil to pay for someone, or did it all end happily ever after?"

"Believe it or not, things turned out okay. Kara's married now . . . to a very wonderful man."

"Do I detect a hint of wistfulness?" queried Nathan.

Carrie thought about it. Yes, she felt wistful, but incredibly, the pain was gone. When had she stopped hurting over Greg? How could it be that she hadn't even noticed its passing? She gazed again at Nathan across the candlelit table. Was he responsible for her change in feeling? Embarrassed, she looked away.

Nathan touched her hand and nodded with a smile toward the

sleeping youngsters. Dusty shared his chair with his orange Winnie-the-Pooh. Mindy was curled in her seat clutching her stuffed Mickey Mouse.

"We should get them home, Nathan," she said softly. "We've sat here for two hours talking."

"And it's been good, hasn't it?" he murmured, taking her hand. "I feel as if I'm just beginning to know the young lady I've traveled with all these days."

Chapter Fifteen

On Saturday afternoon—a brisk, sun-washed autumn day—
Carrie and Nathan took the children to a local park. Carrie spread
out a picnic lunch on a frayed blanket while Nathan set up his easel
and squeezed daubs of watercolor on his palette.

"What are you going to paint?" Carrie asked as she removed
the plastic wrap from a plate of ham sandwiches.

Nathan smiled and murmured, "You."

Carrie looked up, startled. "Me? Are you kidding?"

"No. I want to capture you just the way you look now—your
shining, blue-gray eyes and rosy cheeks, the way your hair catches
the light and caresses your face—"

"Oh, Nathan, please—"

"—the soft pastels in your dress, and even the way your white
angora sweater falls loosely around your shoulders, giving you a
certain—shall we say—angelic quality."

"Nathan, are you making fun of me?"

"No. I honestly want something to remember you by."

Carrie didn't reply. She sensed that Nathan was just as aware
as she of the fleeting, transient nature of their relationship. She
wondered what she would have to remember *him* by—another broken heart and shattered life?

"You don't mind being painted, do you?" he queried.

"I don't know. No one's ever painted me before."

"A pity. They should have. You're beautiful."

Carrie felt her face grow warm. "Shouldn't we eat before the sandwiches dry out?"

Nathan grinned. "Do you really think we can pry Dusty and Mindy off those swings?"

"Not unless we shout 'chocolate chip cookies.' "

"Then I may as well go ahead and paint," said Nathan. He stooped down and turned her face just so, tilting her chin toward him. "Can you hold this pose?"

His touch sent a fresh burst of warmth through her cheeks. "I'll try," she said.

For over an hour Carrie sat motionless while Nathan worked on his canvas, selecting one brush, then another, stroking and daubing, mixing colors with dexterity, then stepping back to scrutinize his efforts.

"When can I look?" pressed Carrie.

"When I'm done. Not before."

Finally she pleaded, "Can I move now? My neck is breaking."

"Very well." He reached down, took her hand, and pulled her up toward him.

She gazed at the portrait, her face flushing with embarrassment. "Oh, Nathan, it's wonderful. But it can't really be me. That's not how I look."

"Sure it is."

"But it's so ethereal, so imaginative, so—so passionate."

"It's the way I envision you—the fanciful, extravagant soul you let nobody see."

"I—I'm flattered."

He mussed her hair teasingly. "Don't get a swelled head. I've seen you in curlers and cold cream, too."

Carrie smoothed her hair into place. "Maybe we should change the subject and think about lunch," she suggested.

Nathan laughed and stretched his shoulder muscles. "I'm ready for more than thinking. I could devour those sandwiches now. How about you?"

Carrie glanced over at Dusty and Mindy climbing on the jungle gym. "Well, the food's ready—if you can round up your two little Tarzans."

That evening, after tucking the youngsters in bed, Carrie fixed a pot of hot tea for Nathan and herself and served it in their compact living room.

"Did the kids give you any trouble tonight?" Nathan inquired.

"Not a bit. They were both dozing before I could say 'roly-poly, pell-mell, tumble-bumble.' "

"I assume you weren't reading Shakespeare."

"The Poky Little Puppy."

"Oh, yeah. The one about the greedy little mutt who gobbles all the rice pudding."

"You've read it too, I see."

"That, *Scuffy the Tugboat*, and *The Saggy Baggy Elephant*."

"Have you always read to the children at bedtime?"

Nathan sipped his tea, then set the cup and saucer on the coffee table. "Not often enough." A distant light flickered in his eyes. "Pamela read to them every night. She adored the kids. They adored her. She shouldered all the responsibility for their care."

"But you're a good father, Nathan."

He grimaced. "I'm learning."

"You haven't exactly had the easiest circumstances." Carrie paused, then chose her words carefully. "You don't talk about it, Nathan, but your grief over Pamela must be very painful."

Nathan sat forward and reached again for his teacup, avoiding Carrie's eyes. "I don't wish to talk about it, Carrie. But I'll tell you this." His voice grew husky. "Losing someone you love—it's the closest thing to hell on earth."

They were silent for a while, lost in separate spheres of memory, until Carrie stood and walked to the kitchenette. "How about some chocolate chip cookies?" she said brightly.

"I thought the kids devoured them today at the park."

"I put some aside this morning right after I baked them."

"Smart girl."

"I do my best."

"Your best is terrific."

She brought over a plate of cookies and sat down beside him. "Help yourself," she offered.

He gave her a glance that was both puzzling and intriguing. "Don't tempt me, Carrie."

She laughed. "Oh, Nathan, surely you're not worried about your waistline."

He reached over and touched her hair lightly. "Carrie, dear Carrie, you're such an innocent. You sit here without a qualm, with me, a seasoned old man of the world."

Carrie absently examined a broken fingernail. "Are you saying I shouldn't trust you, Nathan?"

"I'm saying if you could read my thoughts sometimes, you might have misgivings about this little charade of ours, this daft game of playing house, pretending we're a family."

"But I do trust you, Nathan. Otherwise I wouldn't be here."

"Why should you trust me?" he challenged. "I don't even trust myself." He sighed speculatively. "It's just that I don't know how to read the signals from you, Carrie."

"What signals?"

"I mean, most women would make it clear what they expected. But you give mixed signals. Tenderness . . . then, don't touch! Two steps forward, three steps back—"

Carrie pulled at the jagged edge of her nail. "I really don't know what to say, Nathan."

"You haven't had much experience with men, have you, Carrie?"

She kept her gaze focused on her hands. "I have my Christian standards."

"That's very refreshing. Also extremely frustrating. It's very difficult, Carrie, for a man like me, who's enjoyed a good marriage, to live in the same house with a lovely young woman like you." He chuckled. "You're tensing, Carrie. You don't know how to handle it, do you—the fact that sometimes, however inadvertently, you are very attractive to me?"

She pulled away from his touch. "Stop, Nathan. I don't think we should discuss this further."

"Why not? We want to understand each other, don't we? I'm just trying to be honest with you."

She gave him a sidelong glance. "I'm not sure I'm prepared to deal with your—your—"

"My natural attraction to you?" he supplied. "I imagine not. You strike me as a young lady who has never faced an overwhelming temptation."

"What do you mean by that?"

"Well, for example, if I propositioned you right now, you'd have no trouble saying no. You wouldn't even consider giving in."

"Proposition me?" she shot back indignantly.

He paused. "That's probably a bad example, because if you don't find me attractive, there would be no temptation."

"Oh, but I—I do find you attractive," she admitted. "But you're right. I wouldn't give in."

"See what I mean? You're too good to be true. You don't sin, so it's easy for you. But me, now I've messed things up so many times. I'm running from a murder rap and I've got us all living like fugitives, but I'm too stubborn to stop running."

"God could help you, Nathan, if you'd let Him."

"What would your God want with me?"

"He loves you . . . and wants you to love Him," replied Carrie.

"That's easy for you to say. You're naturally religious."

"That's not so. I know I may seem good to you, and in a way you're right. It has always been easy for me to obey my parents and teachers and be kind to people." She paused, remembering. "In school, my friends considered me a goodie-goodie. Some of them were into drinking and smoking and running around, but I couldn't feel comfortable doing those things. But just because I don't make waves or cause any trouble doesn't mean I don't sin."

"All right, what terrible sins have you committed?"

Carrie reached for the teapot and refilled her cup. "Lots of times I take the easy way out because I don't like confrontations," she said. "Sometimes I don't stand up for what I believe because it's easier to say nothing. I guess if I'm really honest about it, most of the time I do what I please rather than trying to find out what God wants me to do."

"Wanting to do as you please doesn't sound so bad," observed Nathan, "as long as you don't hurt anyone."

Carrie sipped her tea, then looked seriously at Nathan. "Doing what I pleased nearly wrecked my life," she confessed.

Nathan helped himself to another cookie, then sat back comfortably. "What drastic thing did you do?"

"I loved someone once . . ."

"Now that's really sinning," he said cynically.

"You don't understand. Because Greg was what I considered a 'perfect' Christian, I assumed God wanted us together. But He didn't, and I'm still learning to accept His will in that. In that sense, I guess I'm about as stubborn as you are."

Nathan's brow arched. "As I see it, your sins are only sins because you set such a strict, unrealistic standard for yourself."

"Not really. God's standard is perfection. Because He is holy, He can't condone even the smallest, most incidental transgression."

"But nobody's perfect," argued Nathan.

"You're right. That's just what the Bible says. We've all sinned and come short of God's glory. That's why we all need someone to take the penalty of sin so we won't have to bear the guilt."

"That's where this Jesus of yours comes in?"

"Yes, exactly."

Nathan shrugged. "So?"

"So—God loves you so much, Nathan, that He gave His own Son to die for you, to take your punishment on himself."

Nathan was thoughtful. "You're saying that your Jesus is some sort of stopgap between God and man . . . between God and *me*?"

"Yes, Nathan, the living Christ is your bridge to God—if you accept that and ask Him to forgive your sins. There's no way on earth anyone can be good enough to satisfy God's standards."

"And then I try living by this impossible standard of yours?"

"No. It's a matter of allowing Christ's Spirit to come in and live His life through you."

Nathan shook his head ponderously. "An intriguing bit of hocus-pocus perhaps?"

"Not magic, Nathan. A miracle. Think of it this way," she

suggested. "The only difference between a light bulb that gives light and one that doesn't is whether it's connected to its source of power, electricity. Living a Christian life means being plugged into our source of power, Jesus Christ."

"It sounds like a neat little package," Nathan reflected. "During my mother's final weeks she talked about Jesus like this, but I'm not ready to try coping with God when I can't even cope with myself."

"I won't stop praying for you—"

"I wouldn't want you to."

"Then we agree about that, at least."

He winked. "And what I said about propositioning you—don't worry. I respect you too much to put you on the spot like that."

"I'm glad," she said, adding truthfully, "I thought I knew you better than that."

He smiled wistfully and picked up the empty teacups. "Perhaps on that note we had better conclude our conversation and say good night."

Chapter Sixteen

Declaring Monday their official "work" day, Nathan cleaned out his van while Carrie trudged to the laundry room with a heaping basket of soiled clothes. A thin, fortyish blond, in a snug sweater and designer jeans, was already loading one of the machines. She flashed Carrie a generous smile and said, "Hi. Nice day, huh?"

"Beautiful," replied Carrie, setting down her basket.

The woman eyed her intently. "You sure look familiar. I know. You're the new tenant in the apartment down from mine. I'm your neighbor, Annie Waller."

"Hello. I'm Carrie."

"You're the one with the two cute little kids I saw playing around the pool a couple of times," continued the woman, pushing a wad of chewing gum to the corner of her mouth. "Goodness, you don't look old enough to have kids that age. You must have been a child yourself when they were born."

Carrie busied herself with her laundry, quickly stuffing socks and shirts and jeans into the washtub. "Dusty and Mindy aren't my children," she explained self-consciously. "They're—they're Nathan's."

"Oh, you mean your husband's by a former marriage? Well, you sure took on a big job for yourself when you married him. That's right admirable."

Carrie looked up miserably. "I'm not married," she blurted.

The woman stifled her surprise and touched Carrie's arm sym-

87

pathetically. "Now don't you be embarrassed, dear. I know young people do things different these days than when I married my Tom. Back then, where we're from, living together just wasn't a choice, you know? But I'm broad-minded enough to say live and let live."

Carrie nervously tossed a cup of detergent into the washing machine, pulled the knob, and picked up her empty basket. "Goodbye, Annie," she squeaked, and dashed from the room. She heard Annie Waller call after her, "I didn't catch your last name, honey," but she walked on swiftly without looking back.

When she encountered Nathan in the apartment minutes later, she wailed, "I figured the worst thing would be if people thought we were married, but it's even worse when they think we're not!"

He stood at the kitchen sink, filling a bucket with water. He steeled his jaw but said nothing.

"I felt humiliated, Nathan," Carrie persisted. "Ashamed. Doesn't it bother you that we're living a lie?"

"Of course it bothers me," he stormed back, "but what in blazes am I supposed to do about it?"

Carrie retreated gloomily. "You know the answer as well as I."

Nathan jerked the bucket out of the sink, sloshing water onto the floor, and stalked out of the apartment.

Carrie stared at the cluttered kitchenette—breakfast dishes on the Formica table, leftover oatmeal drying in the pan. Tearfully she pushed an empty cereal box and milk carton into an already overflowing trash sack. The bag split open and corn flakes floated onto the linoleum while a toppled tomato soup can drained a thin red stream toward the living room carpeting. Carrie scurried about, wiping up the mess and brushing away tears as she muttered under her breath, "If only I were back home with Mom and Dad and Danny, I'd have a normal, predictable life again! And I'd be free of all this guilt!"

She would also be free of Nathan. And Dusty and Mindy. But could she ever really be free of them in her heart?

Carrie picked up the torn sack and walked toward the trash bins by the parking spaces. She tossed the bag into a large metal container that reeked of spoiled food and assorted malodorous discards. Holding her breath, she turned away too quickly and stumbled over a stack of newspapers beside the bin.

Her gaze focused inadvertently on a familiar photograph in the national news section of a week-old paper. Carrie's heart lurched as she realized she was staring at her own face—her school portrait. Over the picture, the headline glared starkly: MIDWEST WOMAN ABDUCTED BY ACCUSED MURDERER.

Carrie's fingers trembled as she grasped the paper and ran over to the van where Nathan was scrubbing the windshield. Speechless, she thrust the newspaper at him. He put down his rag, wiped his hands on his Levi's, and took the paper. She watched his shoulders rise and fall as he scanned the article. Then he looked up, his eyes glinting with fury. "Frank did this," his said, his lips tightening. "When the police found all of us missing from the house, he convinced them I kidnapped you."

"But you didn't. I've got to let them know."

"You can't. That's just what Frank would want."

"Then I've got to call my parents, Nathan. They must be frantic with worry."

Nathan gripped her wrist firmly. His gaze was penetrating. "Listen, Carrie, you can't call anyone. We can't let anybody know where we are or what we're doing. It would be too dangerous."

Carrie's eyes filled with tears. "Nathan, I can't let my folks be in pain because of me."

He released her wrist and stepped back beside his van. "Then go home!" he snapped.

"How can I?"

His voice softened. "You can't, Carrie. Not yet."

"But what are we going to do, Nathan?"

"I don't know, I don't *know*!" He glanced around cautiously. "Be careful, Carrie. We don't want to be overheard."

Drawing closer to him, she whispered, "I met our neighbor this morning, Nathan. She said I looked familiar. Maybe she's already seen my picture."

"If she hasn't, someone will," Nathan sighed. "Since it's been in the paper, the news has probably been on TV and radio too."

"I just realized . . . we haven't seen TV or listened to the radio in days."

"That was deliberate on my part," Nathan admitted. "I was afraid there would be news bulletins about us that would upset you."

"You're right. I am upset. I never imagined—"

He lowered his face to hers. "We can't talk about it now, Carrie, but the fact is we can't stay here any longer."

"Oh, Nathan, no. Not another move, please!"

"We have no choice."

"But where can we go?"

He gazed at her. The muscle in his right eye twitched. "Give me a little time, Carrie. I'll figure something out."

Carrie turned away. "We'll have to talk, Nathan. Later. Inside."

"Where are you going?"

"To get my purse. I'm going to the store. We're out of cereal and milk."

"I'm not finished with the van."

"That's okay. I'll walk. It's not far and the weather's nice."

"What about the kids?"

"They're in the apartment, coloring. Check on them pretty soon, okay? Don't let them scribble on the walls."

"They can help me polish the van." He reached for her arm. "Hey, you're not mad at me, are you?"

She looked back wearily. "No, Nathan, I'm not mad. I'm just—oh, never mind."

"We're going to be okay, Carrie. I promise."

"I hope you're right, Nathan."

All the way to the market, Carrie bleakly replayed the day's events. Annie Waller assumed that she and Nathan were living together. (*Aren't we in a sense?* she fretted.) The newspaper headlines blatantly proclaimed she was kidnapped. What would the police say if they knew she had come willingly? Would she be considered an accomplice?

You can get out of this mess right now if you just don't go back, her inner voice reasoned. *Just keep walking. Find a policeman.*

Call home. Tell someone where you are.

"I just can't," she lamented. "I can't betray Nathan and the children."

But she *could* call home. The idea tantalized her. No matter what Nathan said, she owed it to her parents to ease their minds. Nathan didn't even have to know.

There was a phone booth just outside the market. Carrie quickened her pace. Her heart raced with anticipation.

Inside the booth she fumbled with her change purse and dialed shakily. When she heard her father's voice, she cried, "Daddy, this is Carrie—"

"Carrie, thank God you're alive! Are you okay?"

"Yes, Daddy, I'm fine. How are you and Mom and Danny?"

"We've been sick with worry over you. Where are you?"

"I can't explain now, Daddy, but I wasn't kidnapped. I'm fine and I'll come home as soon as I can."

"Carrie, baby, knowing you're all right is the answer to my prayers. You don't know how frantic we've been."

"I'm sorry, Daddy. I never dreamed such a fuss would be made about my going away with Nathan."

"Then you are with that man?" her father probed.

"Yes, Daddy, but it's not what you think. He's a kind man—"

"Carrie, you've got to tell me where you are. The police must be notified. You can't handle something like this alone."

"Daddy, I'll write you a long letter and explain everything. I love you. I've got to go now. Give my love to Mom and Danny. Good-bye!"

After she hung up the phone, Carrie closed her eyes and savored the lingering memory of her father's voice. *Knowing you're all right is the answer to my prayers,* he had said. Never before had he even considered prayer an option in his life. Did it mean his heart was softening toward God? If only she could sit down with him now and have one of their lovely, old-fashioned talks!

By the time Carrie returned from the store, Nathan was preparing to leave. He had showered and shaved and put on a fresh sport shirt and slacks. Taking the groceries from her, he said, "You sure took your time."

"I walked slowly. It was a beautiful day."

"Beautiful enough to cheer you up?"

"I don't need cheering."

"You did earlier."

"I feel better, Nathan. Really."

"Good. I'll be back before dinner."

"Where are you going?"

"Out for a while."

"What for?"

"I have some things to check into. Don't worry." He winked. "I may even come back with some answers for us."

Three hours later, Nathan returned to cold pork chops, lumpy mashed potatoes, and a steaming Carrie. "Where were you?" she exclaimed. "Dinner was ready an hour ago."

Ignoring her consternation, Nathan picked Carrie up in his arms, swung her around exuberantly, and boomed, "Listen to me, beautiful. Everything's arranged!"

"Nathan, please, put me down," she bleated, even though she wasn't totally opposed to the gesture.

He released her and, with a flourish, pulled a white envelope from his pocket. He handed it to her and said, "Go on. Open it."

She removed a travel brochure and four printed forms. "Tickets? What for?"

In his most gallant voice, Nathan announced, "You, my lady, are accompanying me on an ocean cruise to the Mexican Riviera!"

Chapter Seventeen

"It simply won't work," Carrie declared after Nathan had outlined his plan.

"Why not?" he challenged.

"You want us to take a cruise to Mexico, get off at some obscure little port town and just disappear into the interior of the country?"

He folded his arms across his chest and nodded. "That basically sums it up."

"But it's too expensive. How can you possibly afford such a trip?"

"It's worth it if we can make a successful escape and start over without living in constant fear."

She raised her hands dramatically. "So we just lose ourselves in some tropical wilderness—just like that? Nathan, do you have any idea what Mexico is like?"

"Do *you*?"

"Well, no, not really. I think it has just about everything—hot deserts, high mountains, steamy jungles. Can you really picture us as—as Tarzan and Jane, living in some little lean-to and surviving on bananas and coconuts?"

"Papayas maybe?"

"Nathan, be serious! You're talking about our lives, our *futures*."

"I am serious, Carrie. And I honestly think it could work."

"How?"

"We become anonymous middle-class American tourists. Fortunately we don't need passports for Mexico..We just disembark at one of the scheduled ports and allow the ship to leave without us. I trust the law enforcement system of Mexico is less tenacious than ours."

"Why don't you just drive your van across the border?"

"Because my picture is probably posted in every border patrol station between here and Tijuana. But no one will expect me to take a pleasure cruise."

"You're mad, Nathan," she chided.

"No. A bit desperate perhaps. But not mad."

"And what about me?" she said stonily. "Am I supposed to follow along and be your—your housekeeper forever?"

Nathan's soothing voice unnerved her. "You can be whatever you want, Carrie."

"Actually, the question is irrelevant . . . since I won't be going with you."

He looked surprised. "You won't come with us?"

"How can I go with you, Nathan? I never should have come this far!"

He shrugged, as if the matter were not worth discussing and said, "The children will miss you."

"I'll miss them too," she answered glumly.

"Is there anything I can say to change you mind?"

"No, Nathan, nothing." She flounced away from him.

Nathan followed and placed a companionable hand on her shoulder. "Would you consider accompanying the children and me just on the cruise? Then, if you wish, you could return with the ship to the States."

She looked searchingly at him. "Why should I do that, Nathan? It would be foolish, senseless."

"It would give us one last good time together. Dusty and Mindy would be heartbroken if we made the trip without you. Besides, your passage is already paid for."

"When are we scheduled to sail?" she asked, her tone still reluctant.

"Friday morning."

"*This* Friday?"

"That's right."

"I thought you had to make reservations months in advance."

"They had several last-minute cancellations." He pressed the colorful brochure into her hand. "Just imagine, Carrie. Saturday we tour exotic Cabo San Lucas. Sunday, it's Mazatlan, and Monday, lush, tropical Puerto Vallarta. How can you possibly resist?"

She wavered. "You say I can return with the ship, then go home?"

"Why not? By that time the children and I will be far beyond the reach of the U.S. authorities."

"I—I'll think about it, Nathan."

Exultantly he seized her and planted an impetuous kiss on her cheek. "You're wonderful, Carrie!"

His sudden embrace dazed her for an instant. Nathan hesitated. Their eyes met and held. "Carrie—" he whispered. His face bent again to hers.

She stepped back shakily, raising her hand in protest. "Nathan, please—"

He retreated, chagrined. "I'm sorry if I offended you, Carrie. But I'm not sorry I kissed you."

Unthinkingly she touched her cheek. The sweetness lingered. "I—I'll warm your dinner, Nathan."

"It's not necessary." He glanced around. "Where are the kids?"

"Asleep already. We played in the pool this afternoon, so I think the sun and water exhausted them. They had an early dinner and went straight to bed."

Nathan walked over to the stove and dubiously examined his cold dinner. He turned on the burner and waited with spatula in hand until the pork chops began to sizzle.

Carrie joined him. "I said I'd do that, Nathan."

Grinning, he relinquished the spatula. "That's what I was hoping." He took a plate from the cupboard. "You know, Carrie, I think we should keep a low profile this week. If we can just make it through till Friday, it should be clear sailing, literally.''

"We'll have to pack—"

"We may need another set of luggage."

"What do people wear on cruises?" she wondered.

"I'm not sure. Let's look again at the brochure."

"We'll need new clothes—a few things anyway."

"And extras like sunglasses, lotion, deck shoes."

"How will we ever be ready by Friday?"

"We'll do it," said Nathan. "We have to."

"I still haven't said for sure I'm going," she warned.

"You're going," he smiled.

The next three days were a blur of activity as Carrie and Nathan scoured discount stores and shopping centers for clothing, shoes and sundry items. Most of the time Carrie was too exhausted to contemplate her future, but occasionally a blade of apprehension pierced her thoughts and left her trembling. Was she doing the right thing? Or was she only getting herself deeper into an already foolish situation?

The night before their scheduled sailing, Carrie's anxieties rose sharply. She was still wakeful and tossing restlessly long after midnight, so at last she sat up cross-legged on her bed and whispered her prayers into the darkness. "Lord Jesus, I want to do what's right, but it's been so long since I've felt real peace. How can I get back those special times we used to share?"

There was no response except for the steady sound of Mindy's breathing. Carrie climbed out of bed, slipped on her robe, and padded to the bathroom. She needed a private place to pray where she could pour out her heart. She closed the door quietly and locked it, then knelt beside the tub and muffled her sobs in a towel. "Father, I can't stand this wall between us," she wept. "Please help me. What can I do to feel your pleasure again?"

The words came to her, *Obey me.*

"Lord, I want to obey, but I'm so confused. What do you want me to do? Please show me the way."

Then, as if morning had dawned, Carrie saw herself in stark clarity and understood. She had chosen her own way, not God's, when she ran away with Nathan and the children. She was trying even now to help them in her own strength, by her own faulty reasoning. And no matter how innocent her relationship with Nathan, by refusing to avoid the *appearance* of evil, she had compromised her standards.

"Oh, God, forgive me," she prayed. "Somehow I made myself believe that doing wrong could make things right. I should have known you never work that way."

When Carrie finally returned to her room, she turned on the little desk lamp and wrote a brief letter to her parents outlining her plans and assuring them she would be home soon. Then, tearfully, like Abraham holding the glinting knife over his beloved son Isaac, she began to compose a letter to the Downey Police Department. With swift, determined fingers, she wrote:

Gentlemen:

My conscience persuades me to write this letter informing you of the whereabouts of Mr. Nathan Havers, whom the authorities have been seeking for nearly a year. I write not because I believe Mr. Havers is guilty of any wrongdoing, but because I believe he and his children will not be able to live a normal, fulfilled life until he is given a proper opportunity to clear his name. I assure you I was not abducted by Mr. Havers but have accompanied him willingly as caregiver of his children. By the time this letter reaches you, we will be on the cruise ship S.S. Sea Queen in Puerto Vallarta, Mexico. I trust that the matter of his arrest will be handled with as much kindness and discretion as possible. I am convinced that Mr. Havers is guilty of nothing more than a profound love and strong sense of protectiveness toward his two motherless children. I entreat all concerned to give a fair and compassionate ear to Mr. Havers' account of his wife's tragic death.

Sincerely,
Carrie Seyers

Chapter Eighteen

At dawn, before Nathan or the children stirred, Carrie slipped out of the apartment, walked to the mailbox, and mailed her letters. She grieved already for Nathan, for the unknowns that lay ahead, for the part she felt compelled to play in his capture. Yet she felt an overwhelming sense of relief, almost euphoria, for having obeyed that inner urging, the unshakable pressure, to do the right thing. Peace filled her for the first time in weeks.

After much soul-searching, she had decided she would still accompany Nathan on the cruise—not to aid in his getaway, but to offer solace to the children when he was arrested, and to accompany the youngsters back to their grandparents' home. Perhaps she would even be able to put in a good word on Nathan's behalf.

After mailing her letters, Carrie stole soundlessly back into the apartment and returned to her room. She sat on her bed and opened her Bible to Genesis, curious to read more about how God had honored Abraham's faith and spared Isaac. But she stumbled upon an earlier passage that amazed her. Years before Abraham offered his son on the altar, while he was still just Abram, he—like Carrie and Nathan now—had chosen to run away and live a lie. Abram had fled his famine-stricken Canaan for the tempting riches of Egypt. Doing so, he disobeyed God, choosing to trust his own devices rather than the Lord.

One wrong choice led to another. Realizing his beautiful wife Sarah would be desired by Pharaoh and that custom would decree his death, he selfishly forced Sarah to pretend to be his sister. Abram's life was spared, but Sarah was taken into Pharaoh's household to be his wife. Ultimately, God protected Sarah and returned her safely to Abraham's care in spite of Abraham's sinful behavior.

But shades of Sarah's dilemma were upon Carrie now—the guilt and shame of running away and living a lie. Sarah had no recourse except obedience to her husband. But Nathan wasn't Carrie's husband.

Still, Carrie ached for Nathan—for what would be and for what might have been. Did she have the right to lay Nathan on the altar and trust God to spare him?

At last, Carrie put away her Bible and went to the kitchen where she puttered about, scrambling eggs and frying bacon for breakfast. As she turned from the stove, Nathan startled her with his presence. He looked appealingly disheveled in his robe and tousled hair. He grinned sleepily and said, "It does a man good to awaken to the smell of bacon frying."

"It'll be ready in a minute," she mumbled, averting her eyes. A sudden nervousness seized her. Did Nathan suspect—could he possibly guess—what she had done? No, he was whistling happily as he put the kettle on for coffee. Why then did she feel so intimidatingly transparent?

"Today's the big day," he mused, measuring instant coffee into his cup. "Our ship sails at five."

"There's still so much to do," she fretted. "Defrost the refrigerator, finish packing, bathe the children—"

"Don't worry. We'll get everything done . . . together."

"You know, I really shouldn't even be going with you," she said under her breath.

"What do you mean? I thought it was settled."

"I could stay here and close up the apartment, then drive the van home."

"Isn't that already your plan when you return from the cruise?"

"Yes, of course, but there's no reason to postpone the inevitable."

Nathan clasped her arm. "There's every reason, Carrie. The

arrangements have been made, the tickets paid for. And my two children are counting on you. Don't disappoint them now.''

"I'll be leaving them anyway in a few days.''

"Then give them these few days, please.''

Carrie looked intently at him. "You still think I'm going to change my mind and stay with you in Mexico, don't you?''

He smiled faintly. "If only you would . . .''

"Nathan, no, I'm not—I can't—it would be wrong!''

"I won't push the matter now. Just promise me you'll come on the cruise.''

"All right. I'm coming.'' She slipped past him. "Breakfast is ready, Nathan. I'm going to wake the children.''

At three that afternoon Nathan's van pulled to a stop beside the terminal building at San Pedro pier. Nathan unloaded the baggage while Carrie guided the children into the sprawling terminal.

"Where's my Teddy bear?'' cried Mindy, pulling back.

"Here, with your sweater,'' Carrie told her. "Come, we've got to get in line for our boarding passes.''

Nathan joined them minutes later and escorted them through the gates toward the dock. A ship's photographer stood near a large sign proclaiming, WELCOME ABOARD THE S.S. SEA QUEEN. As he raised his camera, Nathan waved him off with a curt, "No pictures today, please.''

The man shrugged and stepped aside.

"Daddy, Daddy, look at the big ship!'' Dusty exclaimed. "It's bigger than the whole wide world!''

Carrie touched Nathan's arm. "It's breathtaking! It looks as long as a city block.''

Nathan smiled. "These ships are marvelous things—compact little cities all of their own.''

Mindy reached for her father's hand, pulling close to him as they walked up the covered gangway to the bustling vessel.

"So many people, Nathan,'' said Carrie. "Are they all sailing today?''

"I doubt it. Half of them are probably seeing someone off. Everyone loves a good bon voyage party, you know.''

"No one's seeing *us* off, Daddy,'' said Mindy.

"We'll have our own party, honey." Nathan steered them down the wide circling staircase to the Riviera Deck. They filed through the narrow hallways until they located their cabins. They were grateful to find that Carrie and Mindy's room was just four doors down from Nathan and Dusty's.

"I wasn't sure what we'd get, taking those last minute cancellations," remarked Nathan.

"Oh, the rooms are lovely, Nathan," said Carrie.

"They're *little*!" complained Dusty.

"Look, kids, we have honest-to-goodness portholes," Nathan pointed out. "We can watch the ocean any time we want."

"It's just water," returned Dusty. "I can turn on the faucet for that."

Nathan swung the boy up in his arms. "It may be just water, son, but you've never seen so much of it before at one time."

After taking a few minutes to relax and settle themselves, Carrie, Nathan and the children returned to the Promenade Deck and found an empty spot near the bow of the ship. They watched as dozens of laughing, giddy, waving passengers crowded against the railing and threw colorful streamers to friends and relatives on the dock. The streamers formed a bright, tangled web spanning ship and shore. Someone handed Dusty a packet of streamers. He grasped a yellow one and tossed it with all the strength he could muster. It fluttered in the air momentarily, then drifted down to the piling below.

"Good try," said Carrie, slipping her arm around the boy's shoulder.

The ship's horn bellowed with a deafening blast, sending a terrified Mindy scurrying into Nathan's arms. Even Dusty stiffened and looked up in wide-eyed alarm.

"Look, kids," said Nathan, "the longshoremen are removing those huge mooring ropes from the dock. Now we'll start to drift a little. And see those little tugboats? They're going to pull this big ship out into deep water."

"Wow-ee!" exclaimed Dusty. "Those funny little boats are going to pull *us*?"

"Just you watch, son."

They nestled against one another and watched in mute fascination as the huge vessel began to move. A cool breeze stirred, whipping the streamers about in a lilting dance. Taut streamers snapped as the ship ebbed out to sea. The people on shore became faceless, pastel blurs; their shouts faded to echoes.

Carrie felt a strange lump in her throat—joy and sadness at once. She longed to savor this special moment with Nathan and the children. She wanted to feel as jubilant as the partying passengers around her. But uppermost in her mind was her letter to the Downey police. On Monday they would probably receive it. And then?

Carrie's reverie dissolved as Nathan touched her arm. "Shall we go to the dining room now?" he suggested. "We're scheduled for the main seating."

"Of course," she murmured absently.

"Can I have a hot dog?" begged Dusty as they entered the ornate, golden-hued dining room with its French impressionistic paintings and softly diffused lighting.

"I want French fries," chimed Mindy.

"Sorry, kids, wrong restaurant," whispered Nathan.

The maitre d', a small, bald man with a handle-bar mustache, welcomed them with a flourish. "Please, you let me know if I be of help to you," he said in a thick Italian accent.

Nathan thanked him, then found their table near the spacious side windows. The linen-draped table boasted four place-settings of china, silver, and crystal. A red cloth napkin graced each plate. A slender bud vase of red roses stood in the center beside the condiments.

Nathan seated Carrie and Mindy while Dusty scrambled into his chair and peered at the assortment of silverware. "I got too many spoons," he declared.

"It's okay," said Carrie. "You don't have to use them all."

"I don't need none," he explained. "I don't eat hot dogs with spoons."

"You're not eating hot dogs at all, young man," corrected Nathan.

A slim European in a cerulean dinner jacket and narrow black bow tie introduced himself as Carlo and handed them menus. Gracefully he shook Dusty's napkin and laid it across his lap. Then he reached for Mindy's.

"I don't wear tablecloths," she protested.

Muffling a chuckle, Carrie read her menu. She scanned the multitude of items, then asked Nathan in bewilderment, "Is all this food just for one meal?"

He nodded, amused.

"I could live on this one menu for a week. How do you ever decide what to order?"

"Close your eyes and point."

"Don't joke. I just might do that."

In spite of Carrie's misgivings over the menu, she relished the feast that followed: Caviar on ice, fresh fruit compote, lobster cocktail, thin slices of prosciutto ham with melon, and a succulent entrée of beef Wellington. Just when Carrie was convinced she couldn't eat another morsel, the lights lowered and the waiters paraded among the tables with flaming cherries jubilee.

"Daddy, the dessert's on fire," Mindy warned, clutching her father's arm.

"It's okay," Nathan assured her. "It's supposed to be that way."

"When my birthday cake caught fire, you got mad and said bad words," Mindy persisted.

"That was different," sighed Nathan.

"I don't want yucky burnt dessert," grumbled Dusty. "I want ice cream!"

"It *is* ice cream." Carrie and Nathan exchanged helpless glances, then laughed.

"Maybe after dinner we can put the children to bed while we take in the sights on deck," offered Nathan. "What do you say?"

Carrie nodded. She suddenly felt bright, animated. "It sounds . . . wonderful, Nathan." She gazed around at the elegant waiters, the fancy tables laden with delicacies, and the exquisitely dressed passengers mingling happily. The romantic surroundings captivated her, touched her with their magic. She felt light-headed, deliciously content. How could she resist embracing such a lovely fantasy world with Nathan by her side?

Chapter Nineteen

After breakfast on Saturday, Nathan appeared at Carrie's cabin wearing a bulky, bright orange life jacket. "Are you ready for the lifeboat drill? We have to be at our emergency station in ten minutes."

"You mean I have to wear one of those?" she protested.

"Haven't you heard? It's the latest fashion sensation from Paris."

"In that case, how can I resist?"

"After the drill, I'll take Dusty and Mindy to the Fiesta Deck," said Nathan. "They have special activities for the children."

"Wonderful. And what is *our* itinerary?"

"I thought we'd play a little backgammon or Ping-Pong. And I intend to try my hand at skeet shooting."

"I'd like to spend some time in the sun and pool."

"We can do that too. And maybe even get in a little shuffleboard. We don't arrive at Cabo San Lucas until this afternoon."

The morning passed too quickly for Carrie. Rarely had she had such fun or enjoyed being with someone as much as Nathan. By lunchtime they were exhausted and sunburned, but exuberant. Nathan picked up the children and joined Carrie on the Sun Deck for a sumptuous Mexican buffet. Then they returned to their cabins to shower and change for their excursion to Cabo San Lucas.

The ship anchored near the rugged rock formations just off the coast of Baja. The view was breathtaking, with granite cliffs overlooking miles of ivory-colored, untouched beaches. Carrie, Nathan and the youngsters rode a swift motor launch to shore, the highlight of the trip for Dusty. Native peddlers greeted them at the sagging wharf, their wares spread on blankets and the hoods of weather-beaten automobiles. Carrie gazed in fascination at the ironwood sculptures, silver rings and bracelets, and woven serapes boasting bold geometric designs. A man with a gnarled face, in cotton trousers and a loose shirt, pushed a wicker basket at Carrie and chanted, "One dollar, one dollar."

She kindly deferred but couldn't resist several large crepe paper flowers and a papier-maché piñata for the children. By the time they returned to the ship several hours later, Nathan's arms were brimming over with Carrie's purchases. "Remind me not to take *you* shopping again," he teased as he relinquished his burdens in her cabin.

"Careful with the onyx bookends," she cautioned. "They're breakable."

"So's my wallet."

"But, Nathan, these were fantastic buys. And you know I spent only a few dollars in American currency."

"Just the same, I think I'll keep you away from the shops and street vendors when we arrive in Mazatlan tomorrow. Remember, our money's going to have to last us a long time in Mexico."

Carrie looked up. "Not *us*, Nathan. *You*. I won't be with you in Mexico."

He gazed at her appraisingly. "You still have a few days to change your mind."

Carrie shook her head. "Nathan, can't we just enjoy our time together and accept it for what it is?"

"What it is? You mean good-bye . . . the end of something that never quite began?"

She felt her throat constrict slightly. "There was never anywhere for us to go, Nathan. At least, not together."

"That's your opinion, not mine."

"What are you saying?"

"Nothing. Nothing at all." His voice lightened. "I'm looking forward to escorting you to the captain's gala party this evening.

I hope we can put aside our differences and have a good time.''

Carrie smiled. ''I'll try if you will.''

In spite of their earlier discord, the evening spun an irresistible enchantment for both Nathan and Carrie. When he called at her cabin before dinner, he was wearing a powder blue dinner jacket and bow tie. She wore a simple pale-rose gown. His gaze swept over her with undisguised admiration. ''You look like a princess,'' he murmured, slipping her lace shawl around her shoulders. With deft fingers he tucked a pink bougainvillea flower in her chestnut hair.

At the captain's ''Welcome Aboard'' party, Carrie and Nathan were enraptured by the colorful folk dancers and the strolling mariachis. As they stood in line to be introduced to the captain, Nathan whispered in Carrie's ear, ''You are the most beautiful woman in this room.''

She wasn't sure whether the warmth in her cheeks sprang from too much sun or Nathan's closeness. ''You are by far the most handsome gentleman,'' she returned sincerely.

Long after Nathan escorted Carrie back to her room and said good night, her mind whirled with lovely music, laughter and romance. She sank dreamily onto her bed, savoring the scent of Nathan's aftershave where he brushed her cheek with a kiss.

Only after she turned out her light and lay alone in the dark did she recall the letter and all it represented. *Oh, Lord,* she wept silently, *already I'm wavering. I want to obey you, but it's so hard. Just when I think everything's settled, I feel confused again. I know now that I didn't have to prolong Nathan's arrest. I could have telephoned the police yesterday. They would have picked him up immediately—before our cruise. But I wasn't ready yet to give him up.*

On Sunday morning Nathan accompanied Carrie and the children to the church service in the ship's chapel. The captain read several Scriptures and delivered a brief message in his formal British accent. As Carrie and Nathan shared a songbook for the closing hymn, ''Eternal Father, Strong to Save,'' she noted that Nathan's voice was strong and blended pleasingly with her own clear soprano. They exchanged glances. *If only it could always be this way*, she reflected, *the four of us worshiping together like this*.

Later that morning they disembarked at Mazatlan, took a taxi into the sprawling city, and had lunch at the Shrimp Bucket restaurant. Then they walked along the white beach, listening to the screech and caw of pelicans and gulls, watching a squall of hungry birds swoop over the water in a ravishing ballet. Dusty and Mindy waded into the ocean, eager to claim briny treasure—shells, pebbles and bits of driftwood.

While the youngsters frolicked, Carrie and Nathan sat on a jutting rock nearby and burrowed their bare feet into the moist, packed sand.

"I enjoyed the service this morning," Nathan said, deliberately casual.

"Did you? I'm glad," replied Carrie, feeling anything but casual.

"But I got the impression our captain doesn't know your Jesus half as well as you do."

Carrie stared at him. "What makes you say that?"

"He spoke with such formality and—I don't know—objectivity. Maybe *distance* is a better word. He could have been giving a lecture on anything. There was none of the passion you display when you speak of your relationship with God."

"Some people have different ways of expressing it," she noted.

"No, it's more than that. The captain made religion seem like little more than a ritual. But you're caught up with a *person*. That intrigues me."

"Does that mean you're considering Christianity an option for yourself?" she ventured.

He smiled. "Let's just say I no longer view it with antagonism." He reached for a handful of pebbles and tossed them one by one into the water. "When my mother turned to religion almost on her deathbed, I figured that was fine. Christianity seemed tailormade for the sick and elderly—people who were dying."

"We're *all* dying," Carrie inserted.

"Yeah, well, you know what I mean."

Carrie nodded. Nathan was wearing sunglasses, so she couldn't read the expression in his eyes. But his lips tightened as if he were weighing many serious concerns.

His voice took on a rough edge. "When Pamela—my wife—used to take Dusty and Mindy to church, I told myself I didn't need to go because religion was for kids. That's how I saw it. Old people and kids."

"And now?"

He reached for her hand. "Now I see a beautiful, vibrant young woman who talks earnestly about having a personal relationship with the Lord. It's fascinating. I mean, who wouldn't want to be on good speaking terms with God Almighty?"

"Nathan, are you saying—?"

"I'm saying only that I'm thinking about things I never considered before. That's all." He stood and pulled her up beside him. "It's getting late. We'd better head back to the ship."

"Thank goodness for your college Spanish," she told him. "If I tried to direct the taxi, they'd probably drive me in circles and charge me extra. I might never get back to the ship."

He chuckled. "The only problem is, once the driver assumes I know the language, he rattles it off a mile a minute and I'm lost in his rapid-fire delivery."

She laughed. "You're still ahead of me. My limit is *adios* and *sí*."

After dinner that evening, as Carrie tucked the children into the twin beds in her cabin, Mindy began to weep. Carrie sat down and rocked the child in her arms. "What's wrong, honey? Don't you feel well?"

"Don't go," Mindy sobbed.

"It's okay, sweetheart. I'm just going to meet your father in the Eldorado Lounge and listen to music. We'll be back soon."

Mindy clasped her arms tighter around Carrie's neck. "Don't go," she begged again.

"I said we'll be back," Carrie repeated, gently releasing the child's grip.

"No. You're going away and never coming back—just like Mommy did!"

Carrie looked in astonishment at the child. "Who said that?"

Dusty announced, "We heard you tell Daddy."

Carrie turned her head to hide her unexpected tears. She had so dreaded saying good-bye to Nathan's children that she had mentally blocked out their predictably heartrending reaction. "You're right, Mindy," she managed. "I will be going away soon." She was about to say, *You'll still have your daddy,* but that wasn't true either. By tomorrow they would likely have neither Carrie or Nathan. The bitter reality of the children's plight stunned her.

Groping for words, she cuddled Mindy and smoothed her flaxen curls. "Darling, even when we love someone, we can't always promise we'll be there for them."

"Why not?" Mindy pouted.

"Because sometimes things happen that we can't control. But the love is still there—always there. All your life, wherever you go, whatever you do, you'll carry with you your mother's love and your daddy's love and my love."

"Even if you're not with us?" Dusty asked.

"That's right."

Mindy gazed at Carrie with soulful eyes. "But who will hold me and wash my scratches and tie bows in my hair?"

"And who will read us *Winnie-the-Pooh* and *Poky Little Puppy?*" echoed Dusty.

Unbidden tears flowed down Carrie's cheeks. "I wish it could be me, darlings. I wish I could always do the things for you a mother does."

"You can, Carrie," Dusty stated. "You can marry our daddy and be our mommy."

"I can't do that, Dusty." Carrie reached for a tissue. "But there is Someone who will always be with you—if you ask Him."

"I know," said Dusty.

"Me too," chimed Mindy.

"Who?"

"Jesus," they chorused.

"That's right. How do you know?"

"My Sunday school teacher told me," said Dusty.

"And *you* said so," Mindy added.

"The Bible says so," noted Carrie. "That's what really counts."

"I asked Him into my heart," Mindy asserted.

"Me too. He's right here." Dusty thumped his chest.

Carrie embraced both youngsters, and said, "Then you know what? Jesus will never go away from you, no matter what happens."

"Will He tuck me in bed at night?" asked Mindy.

Carrie stroked the child's hair. "No, honey, but He'll give you beautiful thoughts so you can sleep."

Chapter Twenty

On Monday, after a long, restless night, Carrie awoke with the first rays of dawn. Even as she dressed, a sense of foreboding weighed heavily on her. The apprehension persisted—an irritant, a foreign entity lodged in her mind. *My letter—the police will receive it today. Will they come immediately? This morning? This afternoon? How will it happen?*

As she brushed her hair in the bathroom cubicle, she whispered an urgent prayer. "Lord, please be with Nathan. Protect him. Help him clear his name. Most of all, let him be set free spiritually!"

Throughout breakfast and later, as they prepared to disembark at Puerto Vallarta, Carrie watched, alert, awaiting the impending confrontation. Surely the authorities would come discreetly and handle the matter like gentlemen. And Nathan—how would he react? She was certain there would be none of the rough-and-tumble, cops-and-robbers type of skirmish. Nathan would go quietly. He would have to understand that it was only sensible to face his accusers and, through proper legal channels, exonerate himself once and for all.

A pressure had started in Carrie's head, mushrooming into a pounding headache. Now, the blistering sun of Puerto Vallarta magnified the pain and pushed Carrie to the verge of nausea. As she walked with Nathan and the children over the rough cobblestone streets of the plaza toward Our Lady of Guadalupe Cathedral, she tried to rationalize away her misery. It was just tension, nothing more.

When they entered the quaint, timeworn church, Carrie swayed.

Nathan caught her and helped her into the nearest pew. "Are you ill?" he asked with concern.

"No, I'm fine, Nathan. It's just too much sun . . . or too rich a breakfast. I'll be all right in a minute."

Dusty patted her hand while Mindy looked on worriedly.

"We can go back to the ship now if you like," suggested Nathan.

She waved them all off. "No, I'm fine, really. I just need to sit a few minutes."

Nathan glanced at his watch. "We have plenty of time, Carrie. Besides, it's cool and pleasant here. Why don't you relax with the children while I take care of some business?"

"Business?"

"Yes, I have some inquiries to make."

"You're leaving the ship today?"

"No. Tomorrow morning, well before she sails. That will give us one more evening with you."

"Where are you going now?"

"To see if there's a vehicle I can rent or buy. I want to line things up today."

Nathan returned an hour later, smiling with victory.

"Did you find a car?" asked Carrie.

"Sure did. A nice little van—not the greatest looking, but it runs."

"And you bought it just like that?"

"Business dealings here are less complicated than in the States," Nathan explained. "American *dinero* works wonders."

"Then there's no turning back for you, is there?" Carrie asked quietly.

"Did you really think I'd change my mind?"

"I keep hoping."

"And I keep hoping you'll change *your* mind and come with us."

"I won't."

"Nor I." He looked intently at her. "Are you feeling better?"

"Yes. Much."

"I thought so. Your cheeks have their rosy bloom again."

She stood and took his arm. "What sights are we going to see?"

They left the baroque church and walked toward a gazebo-style bandstand in the center of the plaza. "Straight ahead is the government palace," Nathan informed her. "To our right is the marketplace; on our left, little shops—*tiendas*."

They passed two-story white adobe buildings with red tile roofs and wrought-iron balconies. Jacaranda trees spilled their rambling branches over crumbling stone walls. Brown-skinned women trudged by, babies bundled on their backs. Girls in black braids and short dresses scurried past, laughing giddily.

At a small, open-air boutique Nathan purchased hand-embroidered dresses for Mindy and Carrie. Then he gestured expansively from the jutting cliffs behind them to the swelling ocean ahead. "What shall it be next?" he quizzed. "A taxi ride to the elegant villas of the rich and famous of Gringo Gulch? Or a leisurely walk along beautiful Mismaloya Beach?"

"Oh, Nathan, let's do it all!" Carrie laughed.

For a few fleeting hours Carrie managed to push her fateful letter to the back of her mind. But at sunset, as they wearily climbed the gangplank to the ship, her anxieties returned in full force. Undoubtedly the authorities would be waiting at Nathan's cabin. Her pulse raced; her temples throbbed.

"I'm afraid this day has been a little too strenuous for you," Nathan observed as he unlocked her cabin door. "Why don't you rest before dinner? I'll take the kids to my cabin so you can get some sleep."

"No, no," she protested. "Let the kids stay here. I'll come with you."

"What?"

"I mean, it'll give us a chance to talk."

"All right," he shrugged.

As Carrie walked with Nathan to his cabin, her ankles weakened at the thought of what—or who—awaited them. What could she possibly say to him in their final moments together?

Nathan stared at her. "Your face is white as chalk, even with today's sun."

"I do feel a little dizzy," she confessed.

"You're ill again. Let me take you back to your room."

"No, yours is closer."

As Nathan unlocked his door, Carrie looked up and down the hall. There was no one in sight. Nathan helped her inside, then paged a room steward.

"Do you have something for an upset stomach?" he asked.

The small Filipino nodded. "We have ship's doctor. Or I bring you Dramamine or Transderm patch for seasickness."

"I just want a glass of water, please," said Carrie. While Nathan ran tap water in the bathroom, Carrie motioned the steward over and whispered, "Has anyone been here today looking for Mr.—Mr. Hampton?"

"Someone here?" puzzled the wiry man. "No, no one comes here for Mr. Hampton."

"You're sure?"

"You expect friends perhaps? Please check purser's desk for visitors."

As Nathan brought Carrie's water, the steward nodded politely and left. Carrie sank back on the bed in a mixture of relief and exhaustion. *No one has been here,* she thought incredulously. *Perhaps the police never received my letter, or it was delayed, or maybe they won't choose to act on it at all. If they come tomorrow, Nathan will be gone. Safe!*

She closed her eyes and sank into a deep, welcome sleep. Then, suddenly, she felt herself being shaken. She opened her eyes in alarm. Nathan hovered over her, his gaze penetrating. "Are you feeling better, Carrie?"

"I—I think so."

"It's almost time for dinner."

She sat up and tried to shake the grogginess from her mind. Her mouth tasted like plaster. Then, as her thoughts cleared, she was startled to realize she had fallen asleep in Nathan's cabin.

"I'm sorry," she stammered, "for going to sleep like that. Believe me, it's not the company."

"I didn't mind. You were tired."

"Still, I feel embarrassed."

"If you must know, I enjoyed watching you sleep."

"Now I'm really embarrassed!"

He gave her a bittersweet smile. "I kept thinking how hard it's going to be to let you go."

"Nathan, please—"

"It's not too late to change your mind, Carrie."

She stood up and smoothed her skirt. "I've got to go shower and change, Nathan."

"I'll be by for you and the children in a half hour."

"Make it forty-five minutes and I'll be ready."

Later that evening, after Carrie tucked the youngsters in bed, she and Nathan strolled on the Promenade Deck in the Pacific moonlight. They watched the green and yellow lights of Puerto Vallarta gleam like jewels on black velvet. The moon cast its shimmering watershine across the darkened sea.

"The night is so lovely," mused Carrie.

"Peaceful," observed Nathan. "Stark contrast to the swarming, beehive atmosphere of day."

"The fish smells are stronger at night."

"Does it bother you? We can go inside."

"No, I love it out here, away from the noise and crowds."

"You must be feeling better."

"I am. These cool breezes clear my mind and make me feel like I've been washed clean."

Nathan slipped his arm around her waist. "You had me worried today."

"I'm sorry. I wanted our last day together to be perfect."

"So did I. It almost was."

"I suppose we won't have much chance to talk tomorrow."

"No. I'll be leaving with the children promptly after breakfast."

A lump was forming in Carrie's throat. "I'm going to miss you all," she confessed.

"We'll miss you more than I can say," he said wistfully. His voice took on a resonance she hadn't heard before. "After Pamela died, I thought my life was over. I never expected to be able to look at another woman and feel anything. But you changed that for me, Carrie."

She gazed at him, studying the way the lights and shadows fell across his face. "You know, you've never talked to me about Pamela or her death."

His lips tightened. "Putting words to something gives it a reality of its own."

"Perhaps it's a reality you need to face."

"I suppose it is. And I guess I owe you the entire story—you've been so loyal and trusting through all of this."

"And it may help you to share it, Nathan. It may lessen the burden."

He leaned against the railing and stared out at the distant, twinkling lights. "Pamela and I were deeply in love," he began. "I don't mean just *comfortably* in love. We adored each other. She was a vibrant woman with blond hair, light green eyes, a gorgeous smile and the whitest teeth you ever saw. She was witty and creative, a wonderful wife and mother."

"There was—no other man in her life?" Carrie asked tentatively.

Nathan looked curiously at her. "Why would you think that?"

"Something Frank said—"

Nathan scoffed. "Frank is the most possessive man I've ever seen. He doted on Pamela. No man was good enough for his sister. He and I never got along. Nothing Pamela or I could do would convince him she was happy with me."

"Why is he so convinced you killed her?"

Nathan shrugged. "I suppose losing her made him go off the deep end. Plus the fact that he already hated me for—as he saw it—ruining her life. I'm sure he sincerely believes I killed her, but he's sincerely wrong."

"I know," agreed Carrie.

"Then you have no doubts about my innocence?"

"None. I believe you could go home today and clear your name."

"Well, it's not that easy. The district attorney is positive he has enough circumstantial evidence to convict me."

"What evidence, Nathan? Please tell me what happened."

He took her hand and massaged it absently. "I don't know

what happened, Carrie. Honest to God. It's as much a mystery to me as to anyone.''

"What do you mean?"

"I mean, the whole thing is senseless. There's no rhyme or reason to it. Life was ordinary, pleasantly predictable—then, bang! Everything was gone.''

He shifted his position. Carrie waited in silence for him to continue.

"It was a Friday night. Dusty and Mindy had gone to their grandparents' for the weekend. I had my own art agency and had to work overtime on a special layout. But I figured when I got home I'd take Pamela out for a bite; then we'd spend a quiet evening together. When I walked in the door, I called her but she didn't answer. The radio was on in the kitchen—she always loved to have music playing—so I went to the kitchen, and—and—'' He put his face in his hands and shuddered momentarily.

Wordlessly Carrie slipped her arms around Nathan and held him, his face against hers. She could feel the wetness of his tears against her cheek.

"I'm sorry. I haven't let myself cry since the funeral.''

"It's okay, Nathan. We all need to cry sometimes.''

He straightened and retrieved a handkerchief from his pocket. "Bear with me, Carrie. I want to finish this.'' His voice broke over jags of emotion. "I went to the kitchen . . . and there on the floor was Pamela. At first I thought she had fallen and struck her head. I knelt to help her up, but when I looked into her eyes—'' His shoulders heaved with a sob. "I knew she was dead. But I couldn't figure out how. What had happened? She was too young for a heart attack or stroke.''

"What did you do?"

"I don't know. I went kind of crazy. I started crying, hysterical like. I picked her up in my arms. She was still warm. I guess I thought if I held her close enough she'd come back to me.''

"Did you call for help?"

"No. While I was still standing there with her in my arms, the police arrived. The door was unlocked. They knocked once, then burst in and found me with Pamela. I was too incoherent from shock to realize how it looked. They said they had received an anonymous tip about a terrible disturbance at my address. The caller said it sounded like someone was being killed.''

"Oh, Nathan, no. Didn't they check to see if someone had broken in or disturbed anything?''

"Of course they did. Everything was in order. There was no evidence of a break-in, no sign of a struggle. They surmised that whoever killed Pamela was someone she knew and trusted.''

"Did your neighbors see or hear anything?''

"They supported the caller's report. They heard what they supposed to be a family argument, and one lady even heard a scream.''

"Did they hear anything specific or recognize the voices?''

"No. They were certain only that they heard Pamela's voice and a man's. They figured it was mine.''

Quietly she asked, "How—how did Pamela die?''

Nathan stared mournfully out at the sea. "She was strangled, Carrie.''

"And the police assumed you did it?''

"There were no other suspects. Everything pointed to me.''

"But everyone who knew you must have known how happy you were. There was no motive, no reason.''

Nathan grimaced. "I thought that's how it would be. But my devoted brother-in-law informed the police that Pamela and I were not getting along, that he often heard us arguing, and that Pamela had confided to him that she was planning to leave me for another man.''

"But it wasn't true!''

"Frank seemed convinced that it was. He has a peculiar way of believing whatever suits him.''

"And the police believe Frank?''

"They have no reason not to.''

"But it's just your word against his.''

Nathan sighed. "With the circumstantial evidence against me, the police aren't about to take my word for anything.''

Carrie clasped Nathan's arm in dismay. "Then you really don't think there's any possibility you can clear yourself—?''

Nathan embraced her gently. "Oh, Carrie, dear Carrie, do you think if there was even one chance in a million to clear myself that

I'd have run away like this? You may not believe it, but I'm not usually a man to give up a fight. But I am man enough to recognize when the odds are unbeatable.''

"So you think a jury would send you to jail?''

"I was charged with first degree murder, Carrie. In our state it could mean the death penalty.''

"No, Nathan, they wouldn't do that to an innocent man!''

"If a jury brings in a guilty verdict, in the court's eyes I'm guilty, Carrie.''

She began to cry. "It's not fair, Nathan. It's just not fair.''

He held her close. "Few things in life are fair, Carrie. We just have to do the best we can with what life throws at us. I guess that's why I took the children and ran. I figured I owed them a life with at least one parent. I'm not sure it'll ever be a normal life, but they'll always know how much they're loved.''

"Oh, Nathan, if only I'd known all this before—!''

"Would it have made a difference?''

"I would have understood—''

"Does it make a difference now, Carrie?'' Nathan asked urgently. "Will you come with us after all?''

"I can't, Nathan. I wish I could, but I can't!'' An inner voice urged, *Warn him about the letter!*

Even as she groped for words, Nathan bent his head to hers and kissed her tenderly. After a moment, he whispered, "I never thought I'd care for anyone again, Carrie, but I do. I wouldn't even admit the depth of my feelings to myself. "I love you, Carrie. I won't deny it any longer.''

"Oh, Nathan, I love you too,'' she confessed.

"Then that settles it, darling,'' he murmured. "Of course you'll come with us tomorrow.''

"No, Nathan.'' She eased out of his arms and sat down in a canvas deck chair. Nathan took the chair beside her.

"What is it, Carrie?'' he pressed. "What's wrong?''

"Everything,'' she wept. "The whole world is upside-down, topsy-turvy.''

"Is that so bad? That's what love does sometimes.''

She stared at him, at his ruggedly handsome features etched in moonlight and starshine. "You don't understand, Nathan. I love you, but I love someone else more—"

"Someone else?"

"I know it won't make sense to you, Nathan, but Christ is my first love. I owe Him everything. I'm not happy displeasing Him."

Nathan shook his head, baffled. "Carrie, there's no conflict. I respect your beliefs and would never consider interfering with them. But I'm a flesh-and-blood man while Christ is . . ." His words trailed off.

"His Spirit lives in me, Nathan. If you knew Him, you'd know why I can't disobey Him."

"But I'm not asking you to disobey Him."

"Yes, you are. Unless you loved Him too, my loyalties would be split between you."

Nathan knelt beside Carrie's chair and took her hands in his. "My dearest Carrie, you have been so loyal to me, so trusting and supportive in spite of my irascible nature and our frightful misadventures. I tell you this, if you are an example of what your God is like, I would gladly give myself to you both."

Carrie caught her breath in surprise. "You would, Nathan?"

"I only wish I could believe, Carrie."

"You can, Nathan. Just pray and ask for faith to believe. God will give you faith if you give Him your will."

"You make it sound like such an easy exchange."

She pulled her hands away. "And you made it sound as if you were ready to accept Him."

Nathan stood and walked over to the railing. "It's not something I could do just to accommodate you or for the sake of our relationship, Carrie. When I commit myself to something, it has to be for the right reason, and it has to be all the way."

Carrie rose from her chair and stood beside Nathan. "Would you just give Jesus a chance?" she asked. "Would you pray tonight and ask Him to make himself real to you?"

"I can't promise anything, Carrie. But I will think about it. And if I find I can believe as you do, you'll be the first to know."

He drew her into his arms. "No matter what happens, Carrie, nothing will ever change the way I feel about you."

Chapter Twenty-one

Carrie awoke on Tuesday morning with a bubbling sense of exhilaration. Nathan loved her! She loved him. And perhaps this very morning he would come and tell her he had claimed Christ's love for his own.

Carrie rose and gazed out the porthole at the milky-gray dawn. Sky and water blended in murky whiteness, broken only by dusky trawlers spreading ripples over the ocean's gleaming surface. She showered quickly, styled her hair and applied her makeup carefully. Then she coaxed a sleepy-eyed Mindy out of bed by blowing in her ear and kissing her nose. Half awake, Mindy circled Carrie's neck with her arms and gave her a big bear hug. Carrie held the child, dreaming what it would be like if she were her own. Finally she lifted her to the floor, and reached for the hand-embroidered dresses Nathan had bought them.

"We look like twins," said Mindy, taking her hand as they walked down the hall to Nathan's cabin.

"Yes, we certainly do, sweet—" Carrie's words broke off abruptly. From a distance she spotted several uniformed men at Nathan's door. Her heart leapt in horror. "Oh, no, not now!" she breathed.

"You're squeezing my hand too tight," Mindy chided.

"I'm sorry," Carrie murmured. Her eyes remained on the strangers ahead. One tall, gaunt-faced Mexican gentleman in a conservative business suit stood in the doorway, speaking to Nathan. Behind him stood what appeared to be three Mexican soldiers in blue military uniforms, shouldering automatic rifles.

Carrie's heart pounded furiously as she approached the men. She could see Nathan's face now. He looked stunned. She slipped to his side and looked up beseechingly. "What's happening, Nathan?"

His eyes were dark, inscrutable. "They're here to arrest me, Carrie."

She clasped his arm protectively and challenged, "You aren't American police. What right do you have—?"

The tall man nodded politely. "Señorita, I am Port Agent Juan Gomez. Your government has solicited the aid of our Mexican police, our *federales*. Our orders are to deliver Mr. Nathan Havers to the American border. Since these men do not speak English, I am serving as interpreter. Are you Mr. Havers' companion?"

"I'm traveling with him and his children, yes."

"You are . . . Catherine Seyers?"

"That's right."

The port agent examined several pages of an official form, then looked soberly at Carrie. "We have instructions to take you and the two Havers children into protective custody."

"You mean I'm being arrested?"

"That is not for me to say. Your government will decide such matters." The man motioned to Nathan. "Come, Mr. Havers, we have vehicles waiting."

Mindy clutched Carrie's leg, whimpering. Dusty grasped his father's hand and attempted to pull him back inside the cabin. "Don't go, Daddy. Don't go!" he pleaded.

Nathan picked the boy up in his arms. "Don't worry, son. You're coming too."

Carrie began to weep. "I'm so sorry, Nathan. So sorry!"

He reached out a hand to comfort her. "Don't be sorry, Carrie. It's not your fault. If anyone's responsible for this, it's got to be Frank Colbin. Somehow he must have tipped off the police."

Carrie's agony was unbearable now. "No, Nathan," she whispered. "It wasn't Frank. It was me!"

Nathan stared at her in astonishment. "You—?"

"I wrote a letter to the police before we left on our cruise."

As comprehension set in, Nathan's expression registered shocked betrayal. "Why, Carrie?" he demanded.

"I thought if you were forced to clear your name . . ." she began.

The wound was so raw, so exposed in Nathan's eyes that Carrie recoiled, silenced. She would remember that look for the rest of her life.

One of the *federales* took Dusty while another briskly snapped handcuffs on Nathan's wrists. The armed men flanked Nathan, forming a grim procession as they led him down the hall, away from her.

"Come, señorita," said Agent Gomez. "We must be going. We will have someone bring your things."

"I want my blanket," Mindy begged, hiding her face in Carrie's skirt.

"Please, may I get her blanket? She doesn't go anywhere without it."

The man's face softened as he gazed at the sobbing child. "Sí, señorita. Hurry!"

In stony silence, the *federales* escorted their charges off the ship. Nathan was placed in one automobile, Carrie and the children in another. The long, bumpy ride to the U.S. border was punctuated only by occasional conversation between the two *federales* in the front seat. Since Carrie knew no Spanish, all she could do was sit with the youngsters huddled against her. Mindy remained silent, her eyes wide with alarm while Dusty whined, "I want my daddy. Where'd they take my daddy?"

Carrie couldn't respond. She felt paralyzed with disbelief. Her earlier lofty ideals of doing right and helping Nathan clear his name were dashed by this appalling new reality: armed guards, police vehicles, two terrified children, and Nathan—her beloved Nathan—bound and humiliated, wounded irreparably by her betrayal.

At the California border, the *federales* were met by several American police officers and two plainclothes FBI men. The agents, in their casual garb, could have been merely tourists, except for the badges they flashed and their no-nonsense, take-charge manner.

Nathan was spirited away before Carrie could catch more than a fleeting glimpse of him.

A beefy, curly-haired man, who identified himself as FBI agent James Holt, took Carrie aside and explained, "We'll be driving you to the San Diego airport where we have plane reservations for Springfield."

"Nathan's hometown?"

"My partner and I will be escorting Mr. Havers. Two police-women will accompany you and the children."

"Am I under arrest?"

"At this point you're being placed in protective custody for questioning in the Havers case. The district attorney will decide whether charges should be filed against you."

"What is Nathan charged with?" When the agent hesitated, Carrie pressed, "Please, I've got to know."

In a perfunctory monotone, Agent Holt recited, "Mr. Havers had been charged with one count of first degree murder and two counts of child stealing. Of course, he jumped bail and the FBI has issued a warrant against him for interstate flight to avoid prosecution."

"What about a lawyer? Nathan should have a lawyer."

"Mr. Havers may contact his lawyer when he arrives in Springfield."

"He's not guilty, you know," Carrie declared.

"That's for a jury to decide."

"I'm positive. He didn't do anything wrong!"

The FBI man shrugged. "He ran away, didn't he?" Nodding toward a waiting automobile, he ordered, "Let's go. Our flight leaves in two hours."

An hour later, at the San Diego airport, the FBI agents were met by two policewomen. One, a tall, big-boned brunette who introduced herself as Blanche, led the way to the check-in counter. As they passed a row of phone booths, Carrie asked, "May I please call home before we board?"

The uniformed woman appraised Carrie with shrewd, hazel eyes. "You have five minutes, honey. I'll be standing right here beside you."

Moments later, when Carrie heard her mother's voice, she blurted, ''Mom, it's me—Carrie. I'm coming home!'' She broke down and wept, so Blanche took the phone, giving the plane's destination and arrival time. When Carrie took the phone again, her mother said, ''Your dad and I will be at the airport when you arrive, darling.''

''Will you, Mom? Springfield's a long drive.''

''Just a few hours from here. We'll be fine. We'll be there before your plane gets in. And, Carrie, dear, we'll be by your side no matter what happens. We love you.''

''I love you both so much,'' Carrie replied through her tears. The policewoman motioned for her to come, and she finished hurriedly, ''Good-bye, Mom. See you tonight!''

On the plane—a roomy Boeing 747—Carrie sat with Blanche by the window while Dusty and Mindy sat in the center section with Roberta, the other policewoman. She was a ruddy, round-faced matron with warm, crinkling eyes and an easy way with children. Carrie remained silent for a long while, gazing out the window at cumulous clouds and the patchwork landscape below. The children quietly played tic-tac-toe with Roberta. Carrie closed her eyes and prayed fervently for God to bring good out of tragedy. There was more—the wordless yearnings of her heart for forgiveness, restoration, wholeness of spirit. For herself. For Nathan. And for Nathan, so much more she could not verbalize—a depth of grief she could not begin to describe.

Later, as the stewardess served beverages, Carrie summoned the courage to ask Blanche, ''What will happen when we arrive in Springfield?''

The policewoman sipped her 7-Up, then said, ''You'll be placed in protective custody and questioned.''

''Does that mean I'll be put in jail?''

''Not necessarily. I suspect, if your lawyer's on his toes, he'll have you remanded to your parents' custody tonight. Of course, the judge may order you to stay in town until after the Havers trial.''

''Will I have to testify against Nathan?'' Carrie asked, aghast.

''I don't know. That's up to the district attorney.''

"But you don't think I'll be arrested?" Carrie persisted.

Blanche looked almost sympathetic. "It is a possibility, Miss Seyers. You could be charged with aiding and abetting a criminal. But personally, I doubt if the case would ever be brought to trial."

"But Nathan—he'll be put in jail—?"

"Yes. And he'll stand trial. More than that I can't tell you."

"Can you tell me what will happen to his children?"

"They'll be placed in a foster home until a judge can make a permanent decision about their future."

Carrie put her face in her hands. *How could all our lives have been shattered so suddenly?* she lamented. She already knew the answer, but it came afresh with jolting impact: *We were on a collision course all along—Nathan running from man, running from God. And I went along for the ride!*

Three hours later, when they deplaned at sprawling Metropolitan Airport, Carrie quickly spotted her parents in the throng. Her mother, Lynn Seyers, was wearing a familiar tailored suit and striped silk scarf. Her golden brown hair was curled smartly, framing her attractive face. Carrie's father, Wilson Seyers, stood a little taller than his wife, his thinning auburn-blond hair accenting an oval face with pleasant, ordinary features. His gray eyes glinted with unshed tears when his gaze met Carrie's. She darted through the crowd and embraced them vigorously.

"Darling, you've had us so worried!" her father exclaimed.

"I'm sorry, Daddy. I never meant to hurt you. I've missed you so!"

Her father kissed her cheek, his tears blending with hers. "As long as you're okay, honey, that's all that matters now."

"Greg and Kara and Danny all send their love," said her mother, slipping her arm around Carrie's waist. "I promised them all we'd take good care of you, sweetheart."

Carrie shook her head sadly. "It's too late, Mom. You can't take care of me anymore. I have to accept responsibility for my own life now."

"I know, honey, but if there's anything we can do—"

"Milt Jameson came with us, Carrie," interjected her father. "You remember him."

"Our family lawyer?"

"Yes. He's going to resolve this whole mess for you."

Carrie squeezed her father's hand. Her lower lip trembled. "Oh, Daddy, only God himself can resolve things now."

He rubbed his chin in a meditative gesture. "Yes, I know what you're saying. I'm becoming more aware of that fact all the time."

She studied him intently. "Are you really, Daddy?"

He managed a wan smile. "Isn't that what you've always prayed for?"

"I've prayed the same thing for you that I'm praying now for Nathan—faith in Jesus."

Awkwardly he said, "I'm not there yet, honey, but I'm inching closer."

Carrie hugged him impulsively, then looked over at the two policewomen standing a few feet away with Dusty and Mindy. "I have to go with them, Daddy. They say the police want to question me."

Wilson followed her gaze and nodded. "I expected that, Carrie. We'll follow you over to the station in our car."

She took his arm. "Come, Daddy. And Mother. Before we go, I want you to meet the two greatest little kids in the whole world."

Chapter Twenty-two

Within the hour Carrie was taken to the Springfield police station where she was interrogated late into the evening. The questions were relentless, probing every area of her friendship with Nathan. What had he told her about his past? Had he coerced her into accompanying him in his cross-country escape? How had he treated her and the children? So it went, a maelstrom of questions, one after another. *The slings and arrows of outrageous oppression*— wasn't that how Shakespeare put it? But these barbs were from the lips of strangers who intimidated Carrie with their force, their power, their scathing voices and accusing eyes.

By the time the detectives had finished with her, Carrie felt frazzled, drained, mentally and emotionally battered. They had leveled her with their verbal blows. She was convinced the prosecution would seize upon her words and turn them into lethal weapons to condemn Nathan. Convict him. The possibility turned Carrie's stomach. All the way in the car to her parents' downtown hotel room, Carrie was convinced she would retch. Long after her mother tucked her in bed "just for old times' sake," Carrie lay curled in a ball, entreating the butterflies in her stomach to quiet themselves. They preferred flying in all directions at once.

Butterflies were only the beginning. The week that followed was the most traumatic of Carrie's life. Every day the local newspapers were emblazoned with headlines proclaiming, *Accused*

Murderer Captured on Cruise, Havers Trial Pending, Death Penalty Sought in Havers Case.

Carrie was summoned to the police station several more times for interrogation. She was informed that charges had been routinely filed against her for aiding and abetting a criminal. But several days later, to her immense relief, the district attorney dismissed the charges. He acknowledged, ''A jury would throw the case out of court.''

Carrie tried without success to learn the whereabouts of Dusty and Mindy. She was told only that they were safe in a local foster home. Frank Colbin telephoned her every day at her parents' hotel room, but she put off seeing him socially. He would only remind her of Nathan's dreadful plight.

Carrie attempted to visit Nathan in jail, but he refused to see her. His rejection stung her as deeply as anything ever had. Each time, she returned to the hotel room fighting depression. *What did I expect?* she reflected bleakly. *Nathan must hate me with all his heart!*

Carrie's second week in Springfield brought a new mixture of ups and downs. To her dismay, her parents decided they needed to return home. ''We don't like leaving you, sweetheart, but, remember, we're just a few hours away,'' her mother said, kissing her good-bye.

Her father added reluctantly, ''I wouldn't go if I didn't have a newspaper at home to run.'' He forced a chuckle. ''It'll run without me, of course, but not the way I want it to.''

''I know, Dad. I'll be fine,'' Carrie assured him. ''I hope you understand why I have to stay. Even if I didn't have to testify, I'd want to be near Nathan and the children.''

''We understand, dear. And we'll be back when Nathan's trial begins,'' her mother promised. ''I know God will see you through it.''

''God wants to see Nathan through it,'' she murmured, ''if only Nathan would give Him a chance.''

''We'll be praying for you both,'' said Lynn, squeezing Carrie's hand.

Carrie hadn't minded staying in the impersonal hotel room with her parents, but occupying it now, alone, was another story. Each day she ate by herself in assorted mediocre restaurants, then returned to the unnerving silence of four grim walls. She felt unbearably lonely. She knew no one in town—except Frank Colbin. She had nothing to do, nowhere to go. Her mind was too preoccupied to write anything creative. Her novel had sat untouched for weeks now. Her entire life was suspended in a time warp orchestrated by the Springfield legal system. The wheels of justice moved sluggishly, tortoise-like. There was a grueling pre-trial hearing. Nathan's trial date was set, then delayed. The waiting was misery.

One month from the day Carrie arrived in Springfield, Frank Colbin telephoned with good news. "The children have been returned to my parents, Catherine. They're home at last!"

"Dusty and Mindy? They've left the foster home?"

"Yes, Catherine. Would you like to see them?"

Tears sprang to Carrie's eyes. "Oh, Frank, more than anything in the world!"

"Fine. I'll come by the hotel tonight and pick you up. I'd be pleased if you'd consider having dinner with us."

"You mean with your parents? Surely they won't want to meet *me*."

"Of course they do. They know how devotedly you've cared for their grandchildren. They don't blame you for anything that's happened, Carrie, and neither do I." He paused meaningfully. "They realize it's because of you the children have come home."

Carrie winced. "Please, Frank, don't give me credit. I just did what I felt I had to do."

Frank's voice grew animated. "Dear Catherine, your words strike a responsive chord. That is indeed why I pursued Nathan with such diligence."

"I don't want to talk about Nathan—"

"I understand. Tonight we will simply have a pleasant evening at home. I promise."

Frank was true to his word. From the moment he appeared at her door, looking less pale and gaunt than she remembered, he was the epitome of charm and solicitude. "I've missed you, Catherine," he told her as they drove across town. "We had such delightful times together, remember?"

"Yes, we did," she said politely. A loathsome memory of her last evening with Frank assailed her, but she pushed it from her thoughts. It wasn't Frank's fault that he prompted such negative associations in her mind. Wasn't he a good, sensitive man—a Christian? He deserved her kindness and respect.

At six p.m., Frank pulled into the driveway of the Miles Colbin home, a neat brick house in a pleasant residential section of Springfield. The autumn breezes were brisk, biting, as Frank and Carrie climbed the cement steps to the small front porch. Even before Frank knocked, the door flew open and Dusty and Mindy piled into Carrie's arms with delighted whoops. They smothered her with kisses, then possessively led her into the living room.

"This is Carrie," Dusty announced with pride.

"She's our friend," said Mindy, hugging Carrie's arm.

Frank stepped forward and said, "Mom, Dad, this is Catherine Seyers."

Lois Colbin, a stylishly dressed woman with natural white hair caressing her oval face, smiled and extended her hand. "Hello, dear. The children have talked of little else but their beloved Carrie."

Miles Colbin nodded, his narrow lips pursed in a tight smile. He was a tall, lean, sober man with an angular face, receding gray hair, and spectacles perched halfway down his prominent nose. As he shook Carrie's hand, he said, "We know these past few weeks can't have been easy for you. We hold no grudge against you for going along with Nathan. We're just grateful you took good care of these precious grandchildren."

"I love them," Carrie said frankly.

Lois nodded. "Well, it's obvious they love you, too."

Dusty tugged Carrie's hand. "Come, see. Grandma made fried chicken!"

Carrie knelt down and looked the boy in the eyes. "That sounds dee-licious, Dusty." She embraced him, then asked seriously, "Have you and Mindy been okay?"

Dusty stared at the floor. "We didn't like it much at that other house."

"The foster home? But the people treated you nicely, didn't they?"

Dusty nodded. "But they didn't belong to us."

Carrie drew both children into her arms. "From now on you'll always be with people who belong to you."

"Will you stay with us, Carrie?" he asked.

Carrie framed her reply carefully. "I can't stay with you, but I'll never forget you. We'll write letters and send pictures—"

"Mindy stopped talking again," Dusty told her.

"Really? But she's talking now."

"I mean, at the other place. She wouldn't talk until we came to Grandma's."

Lois Colbin drew Carrie aside privately. "We talked with a child psychologist. He says Mindy may need professional counseling."

Carrie sighed with concern. "I hope you'll let me see her occasionally while I'm in town."

"Certainly. We'll do anything to help her. It was devastating enough for her to lose her mother, but now, with her father out of her life—"

"But maybe he'll be back soon . . . if he's found innocent."

Lois stared at her in amazement. "There's no way Nathan will ever be free, my dear. If the children are ever to have a normal life, they must consider their father dead!"

"But he hasn't even been tried yet."

Lois frowned. Pain flashed in her eyes. "The people in this town have already tried Nathan and convicted him in their hearts."

"Does that include you and Mr. Colbin?" ventured Carrie.

Lois looked away. "Nathan was like a son to us. We thought Pamela was very happy with him . . . until we learned the truth."

"You mean Pamela told you she was unhappy?"

"Not exactly. But she confided in Frank. He didn't tell us until after her death. I suppose he wanted to spare us."

"I don't think Nathan hurt your daughter, Mrs. Colbin."

"I wish I could believe that. It might make losing her easier to bear."

Before Carrie could respond, Dusty came running over and interrupted with a boisterous, "Come on, Carrie. You gotta meet

Mr. T, my collie dog. Grandpa took good care of him while we were gone.''

"I'd love to meet Mr. T,'' said Carrie, giving Lois a flustered backward glance as Dusty pulled her toward the back door.

"Go on, you two,'' Lois chuckled. "Dinner will hold. Everything waits for Mr. T!''

In the days that followed, Carrie spent many companionable hours with Frank and his family. She luxuriated in being with Dusty and Mindy again, and they thrived in her company. She felt drawn to the Colbins, to their warm, comfortable home, and she welcomed every opportunity to escape the confining walls of her hotel room.

Even Frank seemed to have mellowed. He was less edgy and nervous than she remembered. He no longer seemed so consumed with retribution against Nathan. Or perhaps it was just that, having obtained his goal, sweet victory gave him new confidence.

Whatever the case, Carrie found him immensely more tolerable now. In fact, he was becoming a welcome friend. She and Frank and the children became a foursome, visiting the local parks and zoos, ice cream parlors and pizza houses. There was none of the magic with Frank that she had felt with Nathan, but the social contact kept her mind off the turmoil she had experienced for so long.

One evening, after an exhausting day with the children at the circus, Carrie and Frank relaxed in the Colbin living room, sipping hot chocolate and listening to soft music. Everyone else had gone to bed, so the house was pleasingly still.

"This is the best part of the day,'' Frank said, smiling. In the low lamp light, his complexion took on a rare rosy hue. Tonight his face had an appealing vulnerable quality. He was so unlike Nathan, but he was gentle and caring. Carrie's present frame of mind made her seem equally vulnerable to Frank.

"I must confess, Catherine,'' he said with quiet ardor, "a spark was ignited when first we met that now burns brightly in my heart.''

"You're very kind, Frank.''

"Lovely lady, there's more. I believe our future lies together. Our lives are predestined to blend as one.''

Carrie sighed. "I'm trying to manage life from day to day, Frank. I can't begin to think about the future."

Frank's voice rose excitedly. "Imagine a little home—nothing ostentatious—with the two of us and Dusty and Mindy—a perfect, ready-made family."

"Dusty and Mindy?"

"Yes. It would be the ideal solution. We could take them and raise them as our own. They love us both. And you, Catherine, are so like their mother. I see more of Pamela in you every day."

"But the court placed the children with your parents."

"For the present, yes. But that can be changed. My folks are getting up in years. They can't be expected to manage the boundless energies and high spirits of two young children indefinitely. What better solution than for us to assume that responsibility together?"

Carrie was silent. There was a certain bizarre logic in what Frank said. But could she seriously entertain the idea of a loveless marriage just to provide a home for Nathan's children? "Are you forgetting?" she reminded Frank. "Nathan may come home someday."

Frank's countenance darkened. "He doesn't have a prayer, Catherine. We both know that."

"But he's not guilty, Frank."

"He destroyed Pamela's life. He has to pay. I'll give my dying breath to see that he does."

The ambiance dissolved after that. Frank drove Carrie back to her hotel without another word about their future together.

But the idea caused Carrie to toss restlessly for most of the night. Did she dare consider Frank's unorthodox proposal? She liked him well enough to be friends, but it was nothing like the feelings she had for Nathan. But perhaps that was best—a predictable, down-to-earth relationship without unrealistic expectations. And the thought of having Dusty and Mindy as a permanent part of her life stirred maternal instincts Carrie had been struggling with ever since she met the children. But could they ever be a family without Nathan—the matrix, the center, the core of their lives?

Chapter Twenty-three

The next afternoon, Carrie paid another visit to the Springfield jail. This time, to her astonishment, Nathan agreed to see her. She was escorted to a dingy waiting room where several women sat in stone-faced silence. A half hour later, after being routinely searched, she was led to a wide gray room divided by a mesh partition with a counter and chairs on each side.

"You mean I have to talk to him through that net?" she asked the police matron who accompanied her.

"Afraid so, miss. Rules, you know."

Carrie sat down in the designated chair and waited with growing apprehension for Nathan. What would she say to him? What would he tell her? That she was a fool to come? That he would be happily in Mexico with his children were it not for her? Her heart pumped maddeningly in her throat. Her hands were moist. Sweat beads dotted her upper lip. *I never should have come!* she despaired.

Then she looked up to see Nathan sit down across from her. His face was obscured by the wire mesh; drab prison clothes concealed his athletic frame. As he leaned toward her, his face assumed its familiar contours. Still, there was a new, disconcerting aspect to his visage, an expression in his eyes that disarmed her completely.

"Hello, Carrie," he said softly.

"Hello, Nathan."

For several moments they exchanged formal amenities, painfully aware of guards, other prisoners and visitors around them.

"I was surprised you finally agreed to see me," Carrie said self-consciously.

Nathan's eyes clouded. "I'm sorry about that, Carrie. I had a lot of things to sort out in my mind. I just couldn't see you until I was ready."

"Does that mean you're ready now?"

"I think so."

She shrugged haplessly. "I don't know what you're trying to say, Nathan."

"There's so much to tell you, Carrie, I don't know where to begin."

"I do," she said. "I want to ask your forgiveness—not for the letter. I had to write it—but for hurting you and the children. I never should have gotten so involved in your life. Then I wouldn't have been responsible for putting you . . . here."

Nathan leaned his face close to the wire mesh. "I don't regret knowing you, Carrie. I want to tell you what's happened since we were together on the ship."

Carrie blinked back tears. "I know what has happened, Nathan."

"No, you don't." He cleared his throat. His voice emerged gravelly, charged with emotion. "After we talked that last night on the ship, I went back to my room and thought about all you'd said. There was a Gideon Bible in the drawer. I started reading it. In fact, I stayed up most of the night reading. A lot of the things you and my mother said in the past started making sense."

"Oh, Nathan—"

"I tried praying, Carrie. I didn't know what to say. I felt clumsy, self-conscious trying to make contact with Almighty God. But I told Him just what you said—that I was a sinner and needed forgiveness and that I wanted His Son Jesus to be my Savior. Then I thanked Christ for entering my life. I told Him He'd have to call the shots from now on because I didn't know what He had in mind for me."

Tears coursed down Carrie's cheeks. "I'm so pleased, Nathan!"

"After I prayed, I felt so exhilarated, Carrie, I almost telephoned your cabin. But I didn't want to wake Mindy. Then, in the morning, I didn't have a chance to tell you. The police were already there."

"Then why have you refused to see me all this time, Nathan?"

Frown lines settled in his forehead. "I was angry, Carrie, confused. At first I ranted against God. I blamed Him. I felt as if He had played a big practical joke on me. Jesus and I had just gotten acquainted and already He was pulling the rug out from under me." His voice softened. "And I was bitter against you, Carrie. I thought you loved me. Then you betrayed me. It took me a long time to realize that real love—yours and God's—can't condone wrongdoing. God had forgiven me, but I still had to face the consequences of my actions. I finally reached a point where I knew I wanted God no matter what happened."

"Nathan, I want you to know—writing that letter was the hardest thing I ever did."

"I know, Carrie. And for the time being I've reconciled myself to"—he glanced around—"all of this."

"Then you're not angry anymore?"

"I realize I have no one to blame but myself. I don't mean the murder charge. I never hurt Pamela. But I shouldn't have run. I thought I could write my own rules—for myself, for the children, even for you. But I was wrong."

They were both silent a moment. Then Carrie asked carefully, "Has your lawyer given you any idea what your chances are?"

"He tries to encourage me," said Nathan, "but I have a feeling he thinks I'll be lucky to get a life sentence."

Carrie bit her lower lip until it hurt. "I hate this, Nathan. I hate it! How can God allow you to suffer for someone else's crime?"

Nathan made a responsive sound low in his throat. "He didn't spare His own Son, Carrie. Why should He spare me?" He pressed his hand against the net. Carrie placed her palm on his.

"Now who's preaching at whom?" she said.

Nathan emitted a half-chuckle. "I don't know the first thing about preaching," he confessed. "But I found a Scripture verse that really hit home, Carrie. In fact, I've discovered that David isn't the only one in the Bible with great things to say. John runs him a close second.''

''What does John say, Nathan?''

''He says, *If the Son shall make you free, you shall be free indeed.* Carrie, I don't know if I'll ever walk free again outside of these bars, but even if I'm not vindicated of guilt on this earth, I've been absolved of my sins in heaven by the blood of Christ.''

Carrie put her face close to the net. ''I love you, Nathan,'' she whispered.

He kissed her gently through the mesh. ''I love you, darling. I always will.''

A policewoman approached and touched Carrie's shoulder. ''Five more minutes, miss.''

Nathan sat back and said, ''Tell me quickly about my children. Have you seen them?''

Carrie explained briefly how, through Frank, she was able to spend a great deal of time with Dusty and Mindy. She deliberately avoided mentioning her frequent dates with Frank or the fact that she had become a regular visitor at the Colbin home.

As if Nathan read her thoughts, he warned, ''Watch out for Frank. I don't say that just because I'm jealous of your friendship with him. It's something else. He's flaky, odd, you know? Pamela worried all the time about him.''

Carrie stifled her surprise. ''I know you and Frank never got along, Nathan, but he seems nice enough—a decent Christian guy.''

''Christian?'' scoffed Nathan. ''Frank's no Christian.''

''But he told me so himself.''

Nathan shrugged. ''The Frank I knew scorned religion. But who knows? Maybe even Frank Colbin can change.''

''I'd better go,'' said Carrie, standing. ''The guard is looking this way.''

''Will you come back, Carrie?''

''Every day, if they'll let me.''

Chapter Twenty-four

Carrie knew now that she could never be serious about Frank Colbin. It was Nathan she loved, would always love, even if he spent the rest of his life in prison. And now that Nathan knew and loved the Lord Jesus as she did, they shared a precious bond not even death could break.

Carrie pondered how she could let Frank know her feelings without hurting him deeply. He had been so considerate of her, so devoted in his own singular way. Would he be satisfied to remain merely friends? Or would he lash out at her and cut off her cherished visits with Dusty and Mindy?

That evening, as Frank drove her to the Colbin home for dinner, Carrie attempted to broach the subject of their relationship. "Frank, we need to sit down together soon and have a serious talk about *us*."

Slipping his arm around her shoulder, he assured her, "And so we shall, my dear Catherine. Sooner than you think!" But he refused to pursue the discussion now. He kept his eyes on the road, a mysterious smile playing on his lips. Minutes later they pulled into the Colbin driveway.

During dinner, as Lois served roast beef and browned potatoes, Frank caught Carrie by surprise when he said, "Mom, Dad, Carrie and I have an announcement to make."

"Frank, what are you talking about?" Carrie said under her breath.

"This," said Frank. He removed a small velvet case from his pocket and set it beside her plate. "Open it, darling."

Carrie shook her head. "You don't have to give me presents, Frank."

"You are too modest, my dear." He opened the box and held it out for everyone to see.

"Oh, my goodness, what a lovely diamond ring!" exclaimed Lois.

"That's pretty!" said Mindy.

"Is it your birthday, Carrie?" asked Dusty.

Carrie felt her face flush with embarrassment. "No, Dusty, it's not. And, Frank, I certainly can't accept such an expensive gift."

"Of course you can! I'm asking you to marry me."

"I thought we were going to talk about this later," she stammered.

Frank gestured expansively. "What better place than in the company of the people I love most?"

"Are you going to live here, Carrie, with us?" Dusty asked excitedly.

"No, children," said Frank. "We'll have our own house. And you'll come live with *us*."

"Can Daddy come too?" Mindy asked shyly.

A grimace crossed Frank's face. "You'll be so happy with us, sweetheart, you won't even think about your daddy."

"Frank, stop it!" demanded Carrie.

Everyone stared at her in bewildered silence.

"What's wrong, Catherine?" Frank asked in bafflement.

Lois tittered nervously, "Surely you consulted Carrie about the engagement, Frank. You didn't just spring it on her tonight."

Frank's expression darkened. "I didn't see any need to mention it earlier. Catherine and I know how we feel about each other."

"No, we don't, Frank," corrected Carrie. "You have no idea how I feel. I—I like you very much. You've been wonderful to me. But I could never marry you."

Frank shoved his chair back from the table and stood up. The muscles in his face contorted as he struggled for control. "It's Nathan, isn't it? He's the reason you can't marry me."

For a moment no one spoke. It seemed that no one even breathed. Carrie felt every eye upon her. Carefully, she said, "I won't marry you, Frank, because I'm not in love with you."

"But you do love Nathan, don't you?" pressed Frank shrilly. "Don't try to hide it. It's written in your eyes."

"Yes. I love him," Carrie nodded quietly.

Frank massaged his temples fiercely. "It's happening again. I can't endure it—"

"Is it one of your headaches?" Lois fretted, going to her son.

Frank appeared lost in his own brooding reverie. "Just like Pamela . . ." he muttered. He pushed his mother away and strode out of the room. The door slammed behind him.

Lois composed herself and sat down, her expression strained. She reached over and patted Carrie's hand. "Don't worry, dear. He'll be back. He just needs to take a little walk and cool off."

The atmosphere was subdued as Carrie helped Lois clear the table. "I never dreamed Frank had taken so much for granted," Carrie told her. "I apologize for spoiling your lovely dinner."

Lois rinsed the plates under running water. "Don't feel badly, dear," she said. "Frank's father and I were as astonished as you by his sudden proposal. Frank's never had a serious girl."

"That makes it all the harder," moaned Carrie.

"He'll get over it." She handed Carrie an apron. "Here, dear, put this over your pretty dress."

Carrie tied on the apron and picked up a terry cloth dish towel. "You do think he'll be all right?"

"Yes. In fact, I think it's a healthy sign he asked you to marry him. All his life he's never paid attention to any girl except his sister. Of course, it was nice for Pamela to have such a devoted older brother, but I worried when Frank didn't make other friends."

"He's still not over Pamela's death," said Carrie gently.

Lois handed her a plate to dry. "I know he's not." Her voice was tremulous. "None of us are. But Frank makes things so hard on himself. He's so sensitive, so introspective. He broods too much."

"I noticed that about him too," Carrie agreed. "He's been so obsessed with getting revenge against Nathan. It's as if those feelings control his entire life.''

Lois wiped her hands on a towel and sighed. ''Frank has always had a tendency to overreact. I remember the day we brought him home. We passed a dog lying dead in the street. Frank was determined we take the dog to a hospital. He couldn't comprehend that the situation was hopeless. Naturally, we didn't stop. Frank sulked for two days.''

Carrie looked at Lois, puzzled. ''I don't understand. The day you brought Frank home—?''

Lois laughed lightly. ''I'm sorry, dear. Of course you don't understand. Frank was adopted. He was five years old when we brought him home.''

''I see,'' said Carrie, marveling. ''Then when was Pamela born?''

''A year later. You know how those things go. You adopt, you relax, and bingo!'' They both laughed, easing the tension between them. ''We all adored Pamela, but you should have seen Frank. He doted on her. Considered her his personal responsibility.''

''He was good with her then? Helpful? Caring?''

''Yes. All of those. And more. He had had a difficult, loveless childhood before we got him. His parents had abandoned him at birth, so he spent his first five years in an overcrowded orphanage. We did all we could to make up for his pain, but Pamela was the only one who could really cheer him. That's why Pamela's death has been such a blow to him, and why he carries such a hatred for Nathan.''

''But if Nathan didn't kill Pamela, Frank is taking his rage out on the wrong person,'' argued Carrie.

Lois dabbed her eyes with a corner of the dish towel. ''If it wasn't Nathan, who else could it have been?''

Carrie shook her head slowly. ''I don't know. But there's somebody somewhere who knows for a fact Nathan is innocent.''

Frank returned at that moment, entering the kitchen abruptly, his face blanched, his hair disheveled. He seemed annoyed, unsettled. ''Are you ready to go home?'' he asked Carrie.

''Yes, Frank. I was just helping your mother with the dishes.''

"But we're finished now," interjected his mother, "so I understand if you must go—"

"I'll get your coat," Frank said curtly.

Carrie said a brief, uneasy good-bye to Mr. and Mrs. Colbin, then hugged Dusty and Mindy yearningly, knowing she might not have this opportunity with them again.

Frank walked her to the car without a word. But once they were on the road, he spoke in a rash, reproachful manner. "Your affection for Nathan Havers is wasted, Catherine. His life is all but crushed, stamped out for good. We'll see what sort of hold he has on you from prison, or from the grave!"

"Please, Frank, it doesn't do any good to talk about Nathan!"

"Certainly it does my heart good to speak of Nathan's coming retribution," he said in a high, intense voice. "Nathan Havers will be punished. I live for that day. I live to see Pamela's death avenged." He glanced over narrowly at her, drumming his fingers on the steering wheel. "What else do I have to live for, Catherine? What else is left?"

"You have your faith," Carrie began carefully, recalling Nathan's assessment of Frank's religion.

"My faith?" repeated Frank, as if the idea were new to him.

"Yes. When we first met, you said you were a Christian."

"Did I, Catherine? Or did you merely assume that's what I said?"

"I don't remember, Frank. You left me with the impression—"

"And you left me with the impression that I had a chance with you, dear Catherine. Evidently we were both mistaken."

As Frank pulled up in front of the hotel, Carrie gathered her things and said coolly, "I suppose this is good-bye, Frank."

"Not good-bye," he corrected, his tone harsh. "The trial starts day after tomorrow. I'll be testifying against Nathan, you know. I'll see you then."

More than ever before, Carrie dreaded entering her empty hotel room. She missed her parents and longed for Nathan's consoling arms. She needed someone to talk with, to share the anguish and confusion she felt. But her parents were miles away, Nathan was locked up, and now she had just closed the door on her friendship with Frank's family. *If only I could have the family without the man*, she mused.

Carrie fixed herself a cup of hot tea and turned on the television. Maybe something light and frivolous would lift her mood. The late-night news broadcast flashed on with photos of Nathan and an update on the pending Havers trial. "Jury selection begins on Thursday," said the announcer. Carrie recalled Lois Colbin's words: *Everyone in town has already convicted Nathan . . .* Carrie snapped off the TV and sat down on the sofa, trembling.

"Oh, God," she said aloud, "I keep thinking things can't get any worse, but they do. Things look so hopeless for Nathan, and now I've turned Frank against me. It seems I keep messing up my life and everyone else's. Please help me. Show me what to do. You're all I have, Lord . . . but how grateful I am to have you!"

Chapter Twenty-five

Carrie's dreams that night were filled with bizarre images of the two men in her life relentlessly accusing each other. First Nathan's face appeared like a faded chiaroscuro print, his features obscured by wire mesh. *Beware of Frank Colbin*, he warned solemnly. Then Frank, his face looming with a chilling bell-jar distortion, intoned, *Nathan Havers is a murderer!*

Carrie sat up suddenly in bed, perspiring. Dregs of the nightmare remained, bitter, ill-boding. Something terrible was going to happen. She sensed it. She was helpless to prevent it.

Or was she?

One fact was clear: One man had to be lying. She would stake her life on Nathan's innocence. But why would Frank lie? Was his hatred for Nathan so great he would manufacture lies simply for revenge? Or was he trying to protect someone? If he loved his sister as dearly as he claimed, why would he protect her murderer?

There were many pieces to the puzzle, but none of them fit. Did Frank hold the missing piece? Carrie suspected that he did. She had to talk with him one more time before Nathan's trial began. She would telephone him first thing in the morning. But would he be willing to see her?

Even before her morning coffee, Carrie phoned the Colbin home. Miles Colbin answered. "Frank's not here, Catherine. He drove the children to school. Is there a message?"

"I need to talk to him."

"All right. I'll tell him."

"There's more. I'm not sure where to begin."

"Please, speak your mind."

Carrie plunged in. "Mr. Colbin, I know you don't want to hear this, but I'm sure Nathan didn't kill your daughter. I'm just as positive that your son Frank knows more than he's telling."

Mr. Colbin's voice sounded dubious. "Do you have some evidence to support such a claim?"

"No, sir. Not yet. That's why I want to talk to Frank. Would you please ask him to come to my hotel room about seven tonight? Don't tell him what it's about. I'd like to do that myself."

"I'll give him your message, Catherine, but I think you're wasting your time."

"I suppose so. But think about it, Mr. Colbin. What if there's even the smallest chance I'm right?"

There was a long silence. Then Miles Colbin responded soberly, "I'll tell Frank to be at your place tonight."

At seven sharp there was a firm knock on Carrie's door. She drew in a quick breath, squared her shoulders, and opened the door. Frank stood before her in a brown suit and mohair overcoat, offering a conciliatory smile.

"Thank you for calling, for asking to see me, Catherine," he said. "You look beautiful, lovelier than I've ever seen you." He entered, silently appraising the hotel room, then shrugged out of his coat and placed it neatly over the back of a chair. "I apologize for last night," he continued. "I was too impulsive. I ran ahead, took you by surprise. I have that tendency, you know, to be impetuous—an eagerness, an intensity of spirit. I should have given you more time. I know in time you'll see things my way." He approached Carrie and placed his hands lightly on her shoulders. "You see, I've calmed myself. I am quite calm, quite accepting of your decision. I will give you all the time you need, just as I gave Pamela. I am a reasonable man, after all. Reasonable."

Carrie stepped back unsteadily. "I have tea, Frank, if you'd like. Hot tea."

"Yes, that would be fine."

"I bought this hot plate so I can heat water and soups and

things in my room," Carrie rushed on nervously. "I hate going out all the time—the crowds and the expensive, tasteless food."

"Yes, I hate that too. The 'maddening throng.' Better to be with just one person you care for intensely."

"I hope you don't mind tea bags."

"Tea bags?"

"Yes. It's not fresh, steeped tea. My mother won't drink anything else. But all I have is—tea bags."

"Tea bags are fine." Frank picked up a coffee mug and examined it absently. "Are you nervous, Catherine, being alone with me in your room like this? You've never invited me in before. This is a first, certainly a pleasant first."

Carrie forced a sound that mimicked laughter. "Yes, it is a first. And no, I'm not nervous. Why should I be? You've always been very proper. Very respectful."

Frank held out the ceramic mug and waited as she poured boiling water into it. "I've always prided myself in knowing how to treat a lady—with genteelness and style. Not crude and heavy-handed, like some men."

Carrie placed a tea bag in Frank's cup. "Like . . . Nathan?"

"Yes, like Nathan."

"Sugar?" she asked. "I just have these little packets."

"One will be fine. Not too sweet." He took his cup over to the sofa and sat down.

Carrie sat at the opposite end, curling her legs under her and taking care to smooth her dress. She sipped her tea slowly, welcoming the hot liquid in her throat and the warm mug against her palms. She was cold with anxiety; her motions seemed sluggish.

"This isn't a bad room," Frank observed. "A king-size bed and this nice little sitting area. Of course, the decor isn't quite to my taste."

"I'm so tired of this room," said Carrie. "It's not like living in a home. Everything stays so transient, so unsettled. You feel almost anonymous. There's no family to come home to."

"I remember that feeling well," remarked Frank, "that feeling of living among strangers, being invisible, lost in the shuffle, your life always in flux." His voice grew vehement. "Your very existence depends on a stranger's whims—''

He caught himself and stopped abruptly. "I'm sorry, Catherine, for going off on such a tangent." He stirred his tea, then said, "Tell me, dear, what did you want to talk about?"

She paused, pacing herself for best effect. "The trial."

Frank sat back and crossed his legs casually. "I see. It begins tomorrow, you know."

"Of course I know. I keep thinking about it, Frank. I have all these questions."

"What questions?"

"About what really happened. I have this feeling, Frank, that somehow you hold the pieces to this whole puzzle. Am I wrong for thinking that?"

"Not at all, Catherine. You realize, naturally, that I'm to be the prosecution's chief witness."

"I know. What I don't know is what special knowledge you possess about the case. What makes you so sure Nathan will be convicted?"

"He will be, Catherine. Mark my words."

"But you didn't see him commit the crime, Frank. It could have been an intruder. It could have been anyone."

"But it wasn't. I know." His eyes glinted malevolently. "You see, Catherine, I was there."

Carrie sat forward, painfully alert. "You were there? When Pamela was murdered?"

Frank's temples moved slightly. His gaze focused on the opposite wall. "I was with Pamela just before Nathan came home," he continued, his voice turning hollow, breathy. "We had a long talk. Then I left and Nathan arrived. I left by the back door when I heard his car in the drive." He looked levelly at Carrie. "I never saw Pamela alive again."

"That doesn't prove Nathan murdered her."

"But it does! Pamela told me she was leaving Nathan, asking him for a divorce that very evening. She said she loved someone else, someone infinitely more worthy of her than Nathan."

Carrie sipped her tea guardedly. "Did you approve of this other man, Frank?"

"Of course. I knew he could make her happy."

"How could you know that? You didn't even know the man . . . or did you?"

Frank's eyes blinked rapidly several times. "I knew of the man. Besides, I trusted Pamela's judgment. I was aware of how badly Nathan had treated her."

Carrie drew in a sharp breath. "You loved Pamela very much, didn't you, Frank?"

"I've made no secret of that. She was my life, my soul. I worshiped her. I would give my life this very moment to have her back."

"There's so much I wish I understood, Frank."

"What do you mean?"

"Your total devotion to your sister. Such depth of feeling is—extraordinary."

Frank made a pleased, guttural sound. "Yes, I suppose it is." His face took on a beatific sheen. "Did you know Pamela wasn't really my sister? We weren't related by blood at all."

Carrie nodded. "Your mother mentioned you were adopted."

"That's right. Pamela could just as easily have been my wife as Nathan's."

Carrie phrased her words with care. "Is that what you wanted, Frank? For Pamela to be your wife?"

Frank sat forward and placed his mug on the table. "The tea is a bit hot, Catherine. It warms the senses, sends the pulse racing. I'll let it cool a bit."

Carrie shifted her position, edging closer to Frank. "You know as well as I do that Nathan didn't kill Pamela. Are you actually going to let an innocent man be punished?"

"Nathan was guilty the day he married Pamela," Frank said testily.

Carrie shook her head. "We keep going in circles, Frank. I know the truth is out there somewhere, but it's so elusive. Something is missing—but what? I think you know the answer."

He raised one eyebrow critically. "Are you sure you haven't put the pieces together, Catherine? You have a keen mind. I suspect you know more than you're admitting."

She put her mug on the table beside his. "I don't know what you're talking about, Frank. If I had the answers, don't you think I'd try to free Nathan?"

He considered that. "I suppose so, Catherine."

She stood and walked over to the dresser. "I almost forgot. I bought some croissants at the little bakery down the street. They have delicious pastry. I remembered how you liked pastry, Frank."

"That was thoughtful of you, Catherine."

"I bought a jar of strawberry jam too," she said, carrying a white sack over to the little coffee table. She sat down and removed two croissants wrapped in wax paper. She handed Frank the jar of preserves. "Would you do the honors, Frank? I never have enough strength to open these things."

He took the jar and twisted the lid with ease. "You see how simple it is?" he said, pleased. "I'm a small man, but I'm deceptively strong. I have very strong hands. Powerful hands. It took years of exercising to build such strength in my hands."

Carrie stared at him. He looked at her, a light of understanding flickering in his eyes. His expression changed rapidly from relaxed conviviality to loathing. In a precise gesture, he set the open jar on the table. "You know, don't you, Catherine?" he challenged.

"Know what?"

"This was a little trick of yours, a test to determine whether I'm physically capable of strangling Pamela."

"No, Frank. It never occurred—"

"Now you see for yourself. I'm no weakling, Catherine. I'm every bit as much a man as Nathan Havers."

"Of course you are, Frank," she stammered.

"Pamela didn't think so." His tone took on a strange dissonance. "She never appreciated me . . . my finer qualities."

"That's not so, Frank. Pamela loved you very much."

Frank's voice grew strident. "She threw me crumbs, Catherine, just as you've done. I was her brother—nothing more. She and I could have been so happy. She should have been mine, not Nathan's!"

Carrie sat on the edge of the sofa, her mind reeling with the implications of Frank's words. Should she continue this astonishing conversation or bolt for the door? One fact was unarguable: She was having tea with a madman!

The telephone on the bedside table jangled. Both Carrie and Frank jumped up, startled. She stepped forward to answer it, but Frank was swifter. He caught her wrist and held it firm. "Let it ring, Catherine."

Hysteria edged her voice. "Please, Frank, it might be important."

"*This* is important, Catherine—our conversation. It's important to both of us."

"I—I think we've talked enough, Frank. I'm tired—and you're—you're hurting my wrist."

He released her with a sharp thrust toward the sofa. She fell back against the cushions. He lunged after her, gripping the back of her neck and squeezing until she gasped with pain. "You are a shrewd woman, Catherine," he panted. "The puzzle you spoke of—you've found the missing piece. I killed Pamela. She left me no choice. She wouldn't leave Nathan. Wouldn't believe she was meant for me—destined to be mine from the day of her birth. I had to take her from him . . . forever."

Carrie stared wildly at Frank. The phone was still ringing. If only she could make contact with whoever was calling!

"What are you—going to do?" she rasped.

Frank's fingers pressed vice-like into her flesh. "It's really quite simple, my dear Catherine. Now that you know the truth, there's no way you can leave this room . . . alive."

Carrie twisted violently in a futile effort to free herself. A spasm of pain shot from her neck to her spine, prompting a wash of tears. "Please, Frank—be reasonable—" she pleaded.

He gazed at her with angry, sullen eyes. A vein in his temple pulsated noticeably. "You underestimate me, Catherine. I am—if anything—a reasonable man."

As Frank's fingers tightened around her throat, Carrie realized despairingly that the phone—her only lifeline to the outside world—had stopped ringing.

Chapter Twenty-six

Carrie clutched frantically at Frank Colbin as, with precise and brutal calculation, he squeezed her throat in a death-grip. "Please—stop," she whispered rawly.

"What is it, Catherine? A deathbed confession? A final request?"

"Yes," she managed.

He relaxed his hold guardedly, but one hand remained on her neck. "What is it, my dear?"

"Tell me . . . what happened."

"To Pamela? You know."

"The details. How? Why?" *Keep him talking*, she reasoned. *Pray someone will come!*

Frank sat back and held Carrie against his chest. He mindlessly stroked her tousled hair as if he were consoling a child. "I never had anyone of my own, Catherine," he began. "Even after Mom and Dad Colbin brought me home from the orphanage, I was still alone. They had each other, you see. I was—extra. Then Pamela came along. She was tiny, helpless. She needed me. I was always there for her. I taught her everything—how to ride a bike and swim and climb a tree."

"She—must have loved you very much," said Carrie, trying to hold back mounting hysteria.

Frank pressed his cheek against Carrie's hair. "Do you remember those days, Pamela?" he said dreamily. "I was the prince and you were the princess. We ran over the hills and through the summer grass with our paper swords. I slayed dragons for you and leveled entire armies in your honor. I lived for your admiration." His tone darkened. "I thought it would always be that way—the two of us together against the world. Why did you let it change, Pamela?"

"Maybe she just grew up, Frank," Carrie ventured.

"No!" he retorted. "She broke our childhood vows. She dallied with the affections of other men. Then came the ultimate betrayal. She married Nathan Havers."

Frank sat forward, his body tensing, his hand growing rigid on Carrie's neck. "I told her again and again she had to let him go. She had to come home. It could be just the way it was before when we were children. I'd forgive her everything. But she refused."

His breathing came heavier. "When I went to see her that final evening, she was alone. I gave her an ultimatum. Leave Nathan and come with me. She told me to get out. She said I should see a—" he spat out the words "—a psychiatrist. Get professional help, she said."

"But you loved her, Frank. Why did you kill her?" Carrie asked haltingly. "Why, that night, after she'd already spent so many years with Nathan?"

"She was going to tell," replied Frank, his voice edged with desperation. "She said she couldn't keep my sickness a secret any longer. That's what she called it—a *sickness*! She threatened to tell Nathan and our parents that very night. I couldn't let her do that, Catherine. I had no other choice. You can see that, can't you?"

Carrie began to weep, trembling uncontrollably.

"She forced my hand, Catherine," Frank said defensively. "She was the only woman I ever loved, the one person I trusted, and she spurned me." Frank's body convulsed with dry sobs. "Why did she betray me, Catherine? Why!"

As his grip on Carrie's throat relaxed momentarily, she jerked free and sprang from the sofa. Instantly, Frank thrust out his hand and seized her, yanking her back. "You want to betray me too, Catherine!" he raged. "But I won't let you!" His hands circled her neck in a vicious stranglehold. She flailed helplessly against his crushing strength.

Can't breathe—God help me! she screamed silently. The room was spinning, going black around her. She was surrendering to unconsciousness. From a great distance she heard a pounding, a hammering that might have been her own terror-stricken heart. Then she heard a voice, a shout transcending a vast, shadowy gulf. A man bellowed, "Catherine, are you there?"

Carrie forced her way back to awareness. Someone was knocking on her door.

"Frank, are you in there? Open up! It's Dad!"

At the sound of his father's voice, Frank wavered. In that instant, Carrie stumbled for the door. She threw it open and collapsed hysterically in Miles Colbin's arms. The older man picked Carrie up and carried her over to the bed. She was coughing uncontrollably. Miles took a ceramic mug from the coffee table and held it to her lips. "What happened, Frank?" he demanded.

Frank's face was ashen. His eyes bulged slightly, giving his expression an odd, strangled quality. "Nothing, Dad," he said thickly. "We were talking about the trial and suddenly she got upset, irrational. She said I mustn't testify against Nathan."

Miles looked questioningly at Carrie. She attempted to speak, but her throat was too constricted. She rubbed her bruised neck and gestured toward Frank.

"Did you two have a fight?" Miles asked.

"You could say so," conceded Frank.

"I was afraid of that," said Miles. "I've felt uneasy since Catherine and I talked this morning. I had a feeling there'd be trouble. Then you were acting so strange tonight, Frank. You kept saying you were going to visit Pamela. When I telephoned, no one answered, so I figured I'd better get over here and see what was happening for myself."

"You shouldn't have come, Dad. This is between Pamela and me."

Miles' face twisted in pain. "Pamela is dead, Frank."

Carrie found her voice at last. "Frank . . . killed Pamela," she rasped. "And he tried to kill me."

Miles' eyes narrowed. "What's she talking about, Frank?"

"Nothing, Dad. She's crazy, distraught. She'll say anything to save Nathan."

Miles Colbin gripped his son's shoulders with a raw intensity. "Tell me, Frank, did you dare lay a hand on your sister, Pamela?"

Frank began to mewl like a cornered animal. "Dad, she made me do it, don't you see? She wouldn't be my princess anymore. She wouldn't come back to me. Remember how it was when she and I were kids—how I took care of her and protected her?" He clutched his father's shirt front. "I waited for her to come back, Dad. All these years I waited. Why didn't she come?"

Frank fell to his knees and doubled over in a paroxysm of sobs, clutching his father's legs. "I didn't want to hurt her, Dad, but she said she was going to tell on me. I couldn't let her tell!"

In a gesture of stunned disbelief, Miles pressed his son's head against his knees and uttered despairingly, "Oh, my son, don't make me curse the day I brought you into my home!" Weeping, he pulled away from the broken, convulsive form at his feet and reached for the telephone. He picked up the receiver and dialed. "Hello, operator?" His voice broke in waves of grief. "Yes, operator—I'm here. This is—Miles Colbin. Please—give me the police."

The day Nathan was released from jail, Carrie was waiting to take him home. In the police station they watched each other raptly from across the room as Nathan's release papers were given a final cursory examination and his belongings were returned to him.

Then, as he strode across the tile floor toward her, a free man at last, she waited with moist eyes and open arms. He had never looked more handsome—tall and dark, with features as perfectly chisled as Michelangelo's *David*. There was something new in his expression—a seriousness, an exposed intensity born perhaps of his prison experiences. Carrie could see in his eyes the look of a man who had endured an unspeakable ordeal.

Wordlessly he swept her up in his arms and held her as if he would never let her go. There was a new strength in his arms, a new tenderness in his kiss as his lips touched hers, gently, lovingly.

There were no bars between them now—no physical bars, no spiritual bars.

"We belong together like this . . . forever," Nathan whispered against her ear.

"I love you, Nathan."

"We'll never be apart again," he promised, his arm circling her waist as they walked through the massive double doors into the sunlight.

Carrie had a taxi waiting. They slipped into the backseat and Carrie gave the driver the Miles Colbin address. Then she settled back comfortably in Nathan's arms. He bent his head and kissed her again, long and tenderly.

"Nathan, please," she demurred at last. "What about the driver?"

Nathan glanced at the scruffy, balding man in the front seat and whispered, "Let him get his own girl!"

Carrie elbowed him playfully. "Nathan, you're impossible!"

"No, Carrie. It's just that it's been so long, so very long."

She eyed him curiously. "What's that supposed to mean?"

He spoke the words against her cheek. "Just when I found out how wonderful it was to hold you in my arms, I lost you. Now that I have you again, I've got a lot of time to make up for."

She laughed lightly. "We'd better save some for later, Nathan."

"Why? Is there a limit, darling? I was hoping for an inexhaustible supply of kisses and hugs—say, enough to last the rest of our lives?"

"I think I can manage that."

"I hope you don't believe in long engagements."

She looked at him. "I don't know. I've never been proposed to before."

"Well, a bumpy taxi in the middle of town isn't a suitable place for a proposal, but for future reference, keep this in mind . . ."

"Keep what in mind?"

He took her face in his hand. "I believe in short engagements."

She smiled. "But I haven't even accepted your proposal."

"I haven't made my proposal yet. But when I do, it'll be with candlelight and music, or with fireworks and the Fourth of July—"

"Not that long!" she laughed.

"Christmas then?"

"I can't wait," she said softly.

"Neither can I. How about Thanksgiving?"

"That's next week!" she protested. "Don't forget, Nathan, I've got another year of college to finish and a novel to write."

"You can do it all—and more—as my wife," he said joyously.

Carrie touched his face with her fingertips. "Nathan, I've never seen you like this before—so exuberant."

His expression grew thoughtful as he replied, "I've never been so free before, Carrie. Legally free before men. Spiritually free before God. It's heady stuff—freedom—like an elixir, a magic potion. Only not magic at all. A miracle."

He was silent a moment, gathering his words. "A man who's been in prison knows what confinement is, Carrie, but much more important, he knows what freedom is. He knows it by its absence in a hundred different ways every day. He misses simple things like taking a walk in the woods, reading to his children, making a phone call."

"Those are things we all take for granted," mused Carrie.

"Not me. Not anymore. I'll never forget that feeling of being confined, Carrie. It changed me. In some ways for the better; perhaps in some ways, for the worse. I don't know. I just know it's something I'll live with for the rest of my life."

"I want to understand, Nathan. I want to help."

"Having you beside me is more than I ever dared hope for," he acknowledged. "I thank God for you—and I thank you for introducing me to Christ. You never gave up on me. Neither did He. Those days in jail were so difficult, so hopeless. But when I didn't think there was any way out, He encouraged me. I love Him! I want to go on loving Him—and you and the children."

Carrie smiled through bright, happy tears. "You don't know what it does for me to hear you talk like that, Nathan, to know we share the same wonderful Savior."

"This is just the beginning, Carrie. We have the rest of our—"

With a sudden veering motion, the taxi driver pulled up in front of the Colbin house and stopped. He looked back at Nathan with a whimsical light in his eyes. "Here's the place, buddy. If you're not ready, I could drive around a coupla' more blocks."

"No," Nathan said, sobering. "We've come to pick up my children. We'll only be a minute. Will you wait?"

"Sure, I'll wait—with the meter running," the driver cautioned.

As Carrie and Nathan climbed the steps to the Colbin porch, the door opened suddenly. Dusty charged into his father's arms, nearly sending him sprawling back down the steps. Mindy squeezed her father's neck and smothered his face with kisses. Nathan gathered up the youngsters and carried them into the house.

"Daddy's home, Grandma. Daddy's home!" Dusty shouted.

Miles and Lois Colbin greeted Nathan with a bittersweet mixture of smiles and tears. "Hello, Nathan," said Miles, his voice tremulous. Carrie noted that the age lines in the older man's jowls had deepened in a matter of days.

Lois embraced Nathan and asked, "Can you ever forgive us for not believing in you?"

Nathan held her at arms' length and smiled. "I'm a forgiven man, Lois. How could I not forgive you?"

She broke away awkwardly and said, "I know you have a flight to catch to Claremont. I'll get the children's suitcases."

When she had left the room, Carrie quietly asked Miles, "How is Lois taking Frank's confinement to Bellwood Hospital?"

Miles' facial muscles twisted as he struggled for composure. "She's still in shock, Catherine, just as I am. But we're managing." He pulled a handkerchief from his pocket and blew his nose.

"Please let us know if there's anything we can do, Mr. Colbin," said Carrie, touching his hand with sympathy.

"Thank you, Catherine, but we already owe you a debt we can't repay. Frank's mental illness nearly cost you your life. If it weren't for you, he wouldn't be getting the help he so desperately needs."

"I owe Carrie a debt I can't repay, either," said Nathan. "She helped set me free in more ways than one. One of these days, Miles, maybe we can sit down and I'll tell you all about it."

Miles nodded, putting away his handkerchief. He hesitated, then said, "Nathan, I hope you won't shut Lois and me out of the children's lives. They're all we have left—"

"You'll always be an important part of their lives," Nathan assured him. "They need their grandparents. I'm the first to recognize that."

"No hard feelings then?" asked Miles.

"No, sir," agreed Nathan. "Besides, Pamela would want us to remain friends for the children's sake. We all want what's best for Dusty and Mindy."

Lois returned and, with a wan smile, handed Nathan the children's luggage. Then she and Miles gathered their grandchildren into their arms for farewell hugs and kisses.

"This time you know where to find us," Dusty assured them.

"Yes, and we will be together again very soon," Lois promised.

Nathan carried the suitcases outside while Dusty and Mindy escorted Carrie down the steps to the taxi. They settled in the backseat, the children first, then Carrie and Nathan.

"Where to now?" asked the driver.

"Metropolitan Airport," directed Nathan. The vehicle clattered away from the curb with a lurch and a sputter.

As they left the city limits of Springfield behind, Dusty looked up earnestly at Carrie and asked, "Are you going to come live with us again?"

"You can share my room like we did before," said Mindy eagerly.

"No, *I* get her this time," insisted Dusty. "Why should she always stay with you?"

"Because we're both *girls*," said Mindy smugly.

Dusty tugged at Carrie's arm. "Is she right? Are you gonna stay in Mindy's room?"

Carrie looked helplessly at Nathan.

"I think it's about time I made my own claim," he said preemptively. "Dusty . . . Mindy, if this lovely young lady will agree to become my wife, she will share *my* room."

He turned to Carrie, ignoring the cramped quarters of the cab.

"What do you say, darling? I love you . . . the children love you. I'm convinced God wants us together. This isn't the romantic proposal I promised you with moonlight and music, but . . . Carrie, will you marry me?"

Carrie responded with a lingering kiss, blissfully welcoming Nathan and his children into her arms, her heart, and her life.